Help Yourself to France

Help Yourself to France

by

JOHN L. FISK

The Pentland Press
Edinburgh – Cambridge – Durham – USA

© J. L. Fisk, 1996

First published in 1996 by
The Pentland Press Ltd
1 Hutton Close,
South Church
Bishop Auckland
Durham

ISBN 1-85821-434-3

Typeset by Carnegie Publishing, 18 Maynard St, Preston
Printed and bound by Antony Rowe Ltd, Chippenham

This book is dedicated to my wife, Jean, and my two sons Robert and Steven, with whom I have spent many happy holidays in France.

Contents

Acknowledgements

I would like to thank the following people:
M. and Mme. Jean-Marc Duprey and M. and Mme. Pierre Détaillé for all the brochures and other information they have collected for me.

Janet Bowers, Anne Smith and Sue Campbell, my colleagues at school who helped me to compile lists of phrases used in this book and who have accompanied me on school visits to France. I would like to thank Janet particularly for helping me to check the proofs.

Maggie Wilson and Richard Townsend who accompanied me on five camping trips to France and also helped organise them.

I found the following publications useful for reference:
Michelin Guides for Normandy and Brittany
La France A Votre Table. (SOPEXA).
Normandy (James and Joan Walling, Harrap).
Brittany (Elisabeth Morris, Harrap).
The Reference Guide For The Traveller In France (French Tourist Office).
Transport in France (Ben Sykes, Harrap).

Introduction

During my career as a modern languages teacher I have organised numerous school visits to France. On more than twenty family holidays my wife and family and I have been the guests of several French families, stayed at numerous campsites in both tents and touring caravans, at youth hostels, *centres d' accueil*, *gîtes* (holiday cottages) and hotels. This wealth of experience has helped me to write what is essentially a practical guide which will help you not only to plan your holiday but will be useful when seeking accommodation, shopping, eating out, going for a drink, motoring, buying souvenirs, reading signs, and communicating with French people. It will also provide good background knowledge and useful phrases for children as they follow their French course at school.

I cannot claim to have covered every eventuality but I have tried to deal with most everyday situations you might meet in France. If you wish to obtain further information you should write to the French Tourist Office, 178 Piccadilly, London, W1V 0AL. They produce an excellent reference guide for the traveller.

I would be delighted to receive any comments and criticisms and would welcome anecdotes about your experiences to include in a future edition.

Planning Your Holiday

♦ *Writing for General Tourist Information*

Most French towns and cities have a local information office, which is called the **SYNDICAT D'INITIATIVE** or the **OFFICE DE TOURISME**. They publish annually information brochures containing town plans, places of interest, a list of hotels, *pensions* (guest houses), youth hostels, campsites, gîtes, restaurants, estate agents, banks and other local amenities. Often there is some indication of the range of prices for accommodation offered.

These brochures are very easy to obtain. You simply address an envelope to the syndicat d'initiative, the name of the town, France. You can set out a letter as follows:

YOUR ADDRESS AND POSTCODE
(*print clearly*)

MONSIEUR

Veuillez m'envoyer, s'il vous plaît, des renseignements de votre ville et de ses environs.
Je vous prie d'agréer, Monsieur, mes sentiments distingués.

YOUR NAME (print).
SIGNATURE

You should expect to wait about a fortnight for a reply but you will be pleased with the amount and quality of the information you receive.

If you are undecided about which region of France to visit, write to the French Tourist Office for general information and

also see the section headed 'Where to go?' p. 15 to give you some ideas.

♦ *Documents needed*

Passport

British Nationals need a full valid passport. The British Visitor's Passport and the British Excursion Documents are no longer valid. Passport application forms are available at the Post Office. When applying for a passport or renewing an expired or lost one, allow several weeks, as the offices are very busy, particularly during the holiday period.

Ferry Tickets

It is advisable to book these well in advance if possible, especially if you wish to reserve cabins on overnight crossings. It is possible to book a ticket with an undated return sailing. If you do this you must check with the port for space on the ferry two or three days before you intend to sail back. If you turn up unannounced you could face a very long wait, especially at weekends.

If travelling by Eurotunnel you can book in advance through your travel agent or by telephoning Le Shuttle Customer Service Centre. Alternatively you can simply buy a ticket at the toll booth on the day you travel.

E111 Certificate

The E111 is issued by the post office free of charge and covers urgent treatment for accidents or unexpected illness. Make sure the doctor or dentist is *conventionné*, which means that he works within the French sickness insurance scheme. After treatment you should receive a signed statement of treatment called a *feuille de soins*. You cannot claim a refund without it. You will be charged for treatment but can claim back about seventy-five per cent of the cost. Along with your E111 form you will find detailed instructions on how to claim. You need not renew your E111 each year. It is valid as long as you live in the United Kingdom. If your children go on a school trip without you they can use the E111. It is convenient to have photocopies made in case any members of your family are on holiday separately.

Travel Insurance

A travel insurance policy, obtainable from most insurance companies, motoring organisations or the Caravan Club will insure you against personal accident, cancellation of your holiday through illness, loss of luggage, money and valuables. This kind of insurance does not cover your car.

Green Card

Although green cards are no longer compulsory you are strongly advised to take one out from your car insurance company. Your normal car insurance will only give you the minimum legal cover outside the UK. Again it is wise to obtain this document in good time. If you are towing a caravan you must tell your insurance company so that appropriate cover can be effected. Some insurance companies issue green cards free of charge, but most request an additional premium.

Breakdown Insurance

You hope it will never happen, but breaking down in a foreign country is a possibility, even with a new car. At best it could be a nuisance. At worst it could ruin your holiday. You can have peace of mind by taking out a breakdown insurance policy which gives you access to overseas emergency services such as roadside assistance, parts and delivery services, legal assistance and emergency credit facilities. You can also insure against unexpected accommodation charges and travel expenses such as car hire. The motoring organisations and the Caravan Club provide an excellent breakdown service which also includes personal travel insurance. It is also possible to hire spare parts kits, emergency windscreens and warning triangles. In the event of a breakdown or an accident the Touring Club De France sponsors an organisation called Secours Routiers Français, who provide emergency telephones about every three miles on main roads and every mile on motorways.

Current Driving Licence

(International licence is not necessary.)

Vehicle Registration Document and M.O.T. Certificate

You should always carry your registration document and M.O.T. certificate. If the vehicle is not registered in your name you should procure a letter of authorisation from the owner. If you are driving a hire vehicle seek the advice of your motoring organisation about the correct documentation. Check before setting off that your M.O.T. certificate does not expire before your return.

Cash, Travellers' Cheques, or Eurocheques

We always take English money, French francs and travellers' cheques. We have found that buying travellers' cheques in French francs rather than Sterling has given a better exchange rate, but you can lose out on the exchange if you change them back into Sterling. Seek advice from your bank about how and when to change your money. Many people now use Eurocheques, which seem very practical. They dispense with the need to carry a lot of cash. It is sometimes possible to cash travellers' cheques at large supermarkets without a handling charge, but beware of supermarkets where large commissions are charged. Check on the charges before completing any transaction. Always keep your travellers' cheque bank receipt separate from the cheques in case of loss or theft.

Road Maps

The best maps of France we have found are contained in the

7

Michelin Road Atlas of France, which contains two hundred and sixty-eight pages of maps covering the whole country at a scale of 3.15 miles to the inch. Michelin also produce excellent regional maps with their distinctive blue and yellow cover. One disadvantage of buying an expensive map book is that it very quickly becomes out of date, particularly with regard to new motorways.

Documents Related to your Accommodation

(Contracts or letters of confirmation.)

Camping Carnet

This document, though not compulsory, provides insurance up to the value of £250,000 for accidents involving third parties whilst camping abroad and is a form of identity card which is widely recognised and accepted by campsites. Some sites require a camping carnet and some allow a discount on the price if you produce one. They can be obtained free of charge through the motoring organisations and the Caravan Club. If you do not have a carnet, campsites will insist on keeping your passport until you leave. You may feel uneasy about this, since not all campsite offices look very secure!

◆ *Checklist of things to take*

Documents

passport	tickets for ferry
letters of confirmation	breakdown policy
M.O.T. certificate	camping carnet
travel insurance	E111 medical cert.
green card	car reg. document
driving licence	G.B. sticker
cheque book	credit cards
Eurocheques	English cash

French currency

travellers' cheques
travel agency receipt

Books and Maps

this guide!!
local Michelin guides
Caravan Club book
phrase book

road maps
camping guides
dictionary
a novel to read

Equipment for the Car

car manual
battery charger
spares kit
tow rope
spare engine oil
headlight beam deflectors
radiator sealant
spare water hoses

first aid kit
tool kit
spare bulbs
spare keys
warning triangle
tyre pressure gauge
insulating tape

Equipment for Camping or for the Caravan

tent pegs and mallet
groundsheet
table and chairs
water containers
gas cylinders
clothes rack
inner tent
wind break
newspapers (to put under mattresses
to reduce condensation)

awning
chemical toilet solution
levelling boards
leg brace
clothes pegs and string
doormat
small extra tent
sun umbrella
electric hook up cable
wing mirrors

Cooking and Eating Equipment

frying pan
tin-opener
colander
fish slice
kettle

potato peeler
corkscrew
tongs
pressure cooker
teapot

pans

glasses

sharp knives

bread knife

matches

picnic box

ice packs

barbecue (coal/lighters)

ice cube bags

cups and saucers

dishes and plates

knives and forks

spoons (large and small)

egg cups

kitchen gloves

food bags

tin foil

For Washing and Cleaning

large bowl

washing up liquid

bucket

Fairy soap

soap powder

pan scourers

bin liners

shoe cleaning equipment

tissues

tea towels

J-clothes

disinfectant

kitchen roll

plastic bags

brush and pan

Food Items

tea bags

soft drinks

sweets

pre-packaged meals

packets of soup

sauces

salt, pepper, vinegar

powdered milk

cooking oil

sugar

baby food

cordials

coffee

biscuits

tinned food

breakfast cereals

jam

marmalade

rice and pasta

baked beans

sweeteners

Bedding (Find out what is provided)

sleeping bags

pillows

blankets

duvet

inflatable pillows

sheets

lilos   lilo pump

Clothing (General advice only)

Flip flops are useful on wet campsites. High heels are not suitable.
Tracksuits can be used for sleeping in and pottering around.
Take light waterproofs to save space.
We never wear socks.
You can use launderettes!
Remember that you are not going for three months!! Perhaps you are!

Personal Items

towels	soap (box)
hair curlers	toothbrush/toothpaste
hairbrush/comb	razor/shaver
shaving stick/brush	deodorant
perfume	shampoo
toilet bag	toilet roll
hair dryer	paper hankies

For the Baby

potty or portable toilet	nappy solution
feeder cup	disposable nappies
bibs	camping cot
feeding bottles	sterilizing fluid
plastic sheet	

Children's Toys

bucket and spade	football
bat and ball	games
comics	books/magazines
story cassettes	personal stereos

Miscellaneous

alarm clock	radio/cassette
favourite cassettes	spare batteries

scissors
pen and paper
diary
thermos flask
coat hangers
beach bag
contact lenses
beach mats
first aid kit

needle and thread
sunglasses
camera and films
safety pins
torch
spectacles
continental adaptor
fishing tackle

Other Items You Think of

_____

_____

_____

_____

_____

Write down the following information to take with you in case of loss or theft

Passport number
Breakdown insurance policy number
Motor insurance policy number and renewal date
Caravan Club telephone number
Travellers' cheque or Eurocheque numbers
Travel insurance policy number and renewal date
Bank telephone number
Car ignition key number
Car door and boot key number

What to do just before you set off

Check the car over
Fasten down all your windows
Cancel milk, papers, bread
Switch off gas, water and electricity
Take all electric plugs out
Defrost fridge and leave it ajar

Lock all the doors
Leave a spare key with a neighbour
Collect plants together
Tell police/friends of your holiday dates
Give someone your holiday address in case of emergencies
Ask your next of kin for their holiday address if they are away
at the same time
Make sure a neighbour can gain access to switch off your
burglar alarm
Put sick bags in the car!

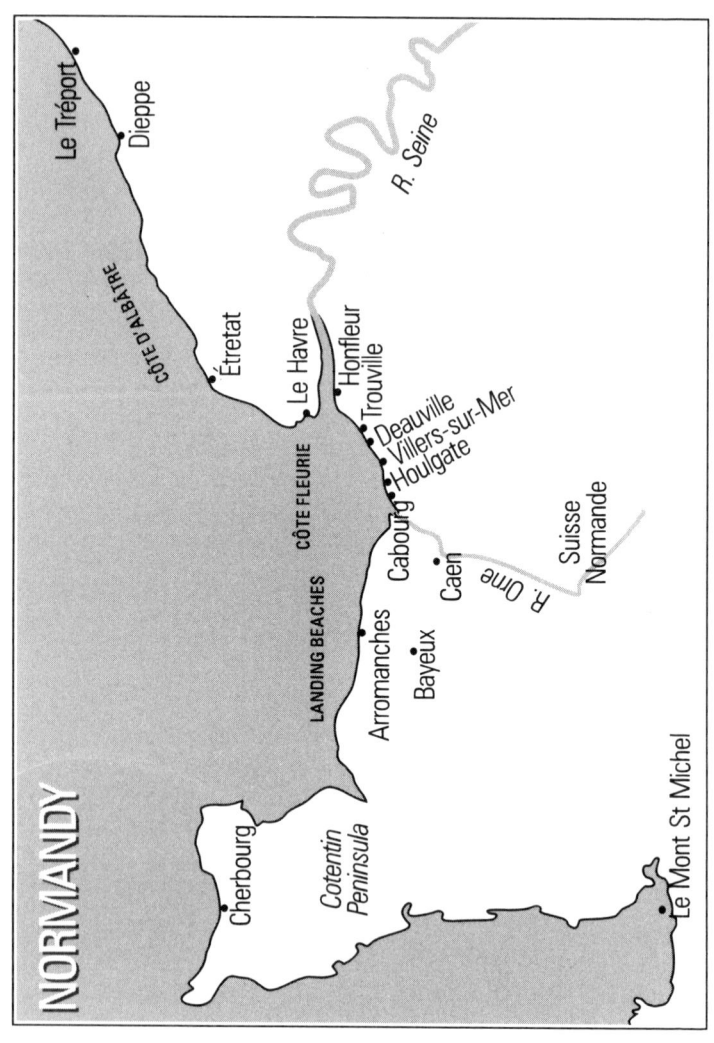

NORMANDY

Le Tréport
Dieppe

CÔTE D'ALBÂTRE

Étretat

R. Seine

Le Havre
Honfleur
Trouville
Deauville
Villers-sur-Mer
Houlgate

CÔTE FLEURIE

Cabourg

Caen

R. Orne

Suisse Normande

LANDING BEACHES

Arromanches
Bayeux

Cherbourg

Cotentin Peninsula

Le Mont St Michel

Where to Go

To explore all the different regions and aspects of France would take a lifetime. It is a country of wonderful contrasts, from fine sandy beaches to medieval châteaux, from high Alpine mountains to lush green meadows, from bustling cities to sleepy hamlets. The problem is where to start. Many British tourists hurl themselves headlong down the *Autoroute du Soleil* and make for the beaches of the French Riviera. Not everyone, however, feels confident enough to embark on a fourteen hundred mile return journey on the first visit to a strange country. The Riviera enthusiasts drive straight past and miss out on many interesting regions which are well worth a closer look. The purpose of this section is to give a brief description of some of the areas which can be reached without a great deal of driving, but which offer a wealth of interest.

◆ *Normandy*

Normandy is made up of five départements: **Calvados, Eure, Manche, Orne** and **Seine Maritime**. One of the most northerly parts of France, it is the region best served by cross-channel ferries and consequently is one of the easiest areas to explore. It is also within reach of Paris. The shortest crossing (approximately four hours) is **Newhaven** to **Dieppe**. From east to west the other crossings are **Portsmouth, Southhampton** or **Poole** to **Le Havre, Caen (Ouistreham), Cherbourg** and **St. Malo**.

Normandy has been involved in two key events in the history of France and England: William the Conqueror's invasion and the D-Day Landings. It was from Normandy that William invaded England in 1066. After the defeat of King Harold at the Battle of Hastings, William became king and England and

Normandy were united. The story of the conquest is told in the famous Bayeux Tapestry, which is visited by many tourists every year. It is housed in a museum in **Bayeux** with an excellent exhibition and video film in English. For further information write to the Office de Tourisme, 1 Rue des Cuisiniers, 14403 Bayeux.

During the Second World War France was occupied by the Germans for four years. On 6 June 1944 the Allies landed thousands of troops on the Normandy beaches, while glider-borne troops and paratroops were landing behind German lines. For the following ten weeks one of the most decisive battles in history was fought, as a result of which Normandy was the first part of France to be liberated. There are two excellent museums within a few miles of each other, commemorating this momentous event; the **1944 Battle of Normandy Memorial Museum** in **Bayeux** and the **Landing Museum** in **Arromanches**, which is situated on the coast near **Bayeux**. Other museums include the **Pegasus Bridge Museum** at **Bénouville**, the **Liberation Museum** in **Cherbourg**, the **Museum of the Poche de Falaise Battle** in **Falaise**, the **Commando 4 Museum** in **Ouistreham** and the **Memorial Museum** in **Caen**. For further information write to the Comité Départemental du Tourisme du Calvados, Place du Canada, 14000 Caen. At **Arromanches**, where the British and Canadians landed on D-Day you can also see the remains of the Allied floating Mulberry harbour which has been left in place to commemorate the landings.

From **Le Tréport** near **Dieppe** in the east to **Mont Saint Michel** in the west there are six hundred kilometres of attractive beaches and cliffs. The Alabaster Coast (**Côte d'Albâtre**) situated above the river Seine is a favourite destination for Parisian weekenders. It is well known for its chalk cliffs. The lovely resort of **Etretat** with its beautiful cliff walks and pebbly beach is well worth a visit. Just below the mouth of the Seine is the **Côte Fleurie**. Here you can visit the old fishing port of **Honfleur** with its harbour surrounded by picturesque buildings and its bustling, unmissable Saturday market. Further westwards are the holiday resorts of **Deauville** and **Trouville** with their excellent sandy beaches and their 'planches' (wooden walkways along the beach) where tourists love to promenade. Other small resorts well worth looking at are **Villers-sur-Mer, Houlgate** and **Cabourg**. To the west of the river Orne whose estuary is at **Ouistreham**, near **Caen** are the Normandy Landing Beaches nicknamed Sword, Juno, Gold, Omaha and Utah and which will always be known by their wartime names. Go westward again and you will arrive at the **Cotentin Peninsula**. This is a 'Land's End' type of region with cliffs and sandy beaches, dunes and rushes. The west coast of the Cotentin is warmed by the Gulf Stream and enjoys more sunshine than the eastern side.

This brings us to the gem of Normandy, the **Mont Saint Michel**, which is situated off-shore where Normandy meets Brittany. Mont Saint Michel is a small islet at the end of a two kilometre causeway on which from the thirteenth century monks built an abbey. There are many picturesque buildings, including shops and museums. The walk around the ramparts offers wonderful views and the speed of the incoming tide is impressive to watch. Mont Saint Michel can be reached by car all the year round and entrance is free. However, it can be extremely busy in summer. An early morning or an evening visit (when it is floodlit) will avoid the crowds.

Invariably, it is the coast of Normandy which attracts visitors, but the countryside inland also has a great deal to offer with its valleys, green copses, beech and pine forests, small villages, country lanes, orchards and rich pasture land. Particularly interesting is the valley of the river Seine with its cliffs and pebble outcrops and its frequent bends. In the valley of the river Orne is '**La Suisse Normande**', where you will see nature in its wild state. There are gorges, high rocky cliffs, thick woods and streams. Wherever you go in Normandy you will see traditional Norman houses with their black or brown and white timber framed clay walls and sometimes thatched roofs.

Another good reason for visiting Normandy is to sample the local food and drinks. Norman recipes are usually quite simple and make use of the local dairy produce and apples. Most of the cooking is based on cream. Norman cattle, one of the most important breeds in France, are excellent milkers as well as meat producers. The sea also has a great influence in the shape of

Dieppe sole, oysters and other seafood. The excellence of Normandy lamb, chicken and duck dishes are matched by that of its cheeses: Neufchâtel, Pont-L'Evêque, Livarot and Camembert. The creamy omelettes of Mont Saint Michel are famous world wide. Also popular are andouille and boudin sausages, tripe and pâtés. Normandy is not a wine producing area but does produce large quantities of cider which can be bought still or sparkling, dry or sweet. A visit to Normandy would not be complete without sampling Calvados, a strong brandy type drink made from apples, and Bénédictine, a golden liqueur made from '*eau de vie*' and local herbs.

For detailed information about every aspect of Normandy you will find the Michelin Green Guide very useful and for general tourist information you can write to the regional tourist office, whose address is Comité Régional de Tourisme, 46 avenue Foch, 27000 Evreux, France.

Normandy really is worth the trouble. For a first visit it is probably a good idea to choose your accommodation in a fairly central position such as **Cabourg** or **Houlgate**, so that you can easily explore the main places of interest by driving east, west or south.

♦ *The Emerald Coast of Brittany*

The most easterly part of Brittany, situated next to Normandy is sometimes called '**Haute Bretagne**' (High Brittany). It is made up of two *départements*, the **Côtes du Nord** and **Ille-et-Vilaine**. The coastal part of the region is known quite justifiably as the **Côte d'Emeraude** (the Emerald Coast). It is a rich mixture of rocky coves, points of land and very good sandy beaches.

The best way to reach this region is to take an overnight ferry (Brittany Ferries) from **Portsmouth** to **Saint Malo**. In this way you can have a good night's sleep and arrive in Saint Malo fresh and ready to make for your destination in daylight. One word of warning, however: you must book early in the year to be sure of a ferry and very early if you want overnight berths.

The weather in Brittany is generally changeable, humid and

mild. In summer it is usually bright but never very hot. It rains slightly more on the coast than it does inland and it has its fair share of overcast days.

The influence of the sea on the area is very great. The tides in the Gulf of Saint Malo are strong and can sometimes reach a height of thirteen and a half metres. At Mont Saint Michel they have been known to reach fifteen metres. Tides come in very fast and care should be taken not to be caught by them. The high tides are responsible for the many coves, tunnels, arches and peninsulas in the region. They have also helped to form the hundreds of fine sandy beaches. You will normally find the times of the tides indicated in hotels, at seaside resorts and in the local newspapers.

The sea also influences the local cuisine. Most restaurants offer *'fruits de mer'* (seafood) menus. The **Saint Malo** area is one of the most important oyster growing regions in the world, with its *huîtres plates* (Belon oysters), *les Portuguaises* (Portuguese oysters) and *les Gigas* (oysters from Japan). At **Cancale**, near Saint Malo, you can visit the oyster beds at low tide and buy direct from the growers on the beach. There is a wide variety of shrimps, prawns, lobsters, langoustes, crayfish, scallops, cockles, mussels and winkles – a seafood enthusiast's paradise.

Brittany is sometimes also known as the market garden of France. The **Côtes-du-Nord** is famous for its potatoes, onions and garlic. It is from here that the onion sellers come to England to sell door to door. It is also well known for its poultry production. The raising of sheep, cattle and pigs provides a very wide range of delicatessen products such as local pâtés, black puddings and sausages. **Fougères**, near Saint Malo, is renowned for its cattle market.

This part of Brittany does not produce any wine, but like Normandy hundreds of thousands of tons of cider apples are crushed to produce apple juice and cider.

Crêpes (pancakes) are a local speciality. A holiday here is not complete without a visit to a *crêperie*, where pancakes are made of wheat flour and served with a mouth-watering variety of savoury and sweet fillings.

Saint Malo is an ideal centre, both as an excellent resort in

19

itself, but also because of its central position in relation to all the other places of interest in the area. It is made up of four towns, **Saint-Servan, Paramé, Rothéneuf** and **Saint Malo** itself, which together form a superb tourist centre, popular with French and English holidaymakers alike. The main attraction is the walled town, which was badly damaged in the Second World War, but which has been rebuilt largely in its original style. At the northern end of the town there is a castle, now a museum, which overlooks the sea. On the western side of the walls is a beach with a narrow causeway leading to the islands of **Grand Bé**. North of the town there is another island, cut off except at low tide, on which stands the **Fort Nationale** which dates back to 1689. There is a regular daily service to the Channel Islands from Saint Malo. Many English day trippers enjoy the contrast between the 'Frenchness' of Saint Malo and the 'Englishness' of the Channel Islands.

Saint Malo is a working industrial port and a fishing port. It has a large harbour for leisure craft and it handles cross-channel ferries. There is a lot to see there for tourists with a nautical interest.

Other tourist attractions include walks around the ramparts, the bustling town centre for shopping, the sea aquarium, the castle museum, the cathedral of Saint Vincent, sea excursions to **Dinard** and **Cap Fréhel**, a trip to **Dinan** along the river Rance, an open air swimming pool on the beach which fills naturally with sea water, and most importantly, the miles of excellent beaches which stretch from **Saint-Servan** down to **Paramé**. Incidentally, there is an excellent **Centre d'Accueil** (similar to a youth hostel) at **Paramé**.

Just across the Rance estuary from Saint Malo lies the town of **Dinard** which you reach by road via the **Barrage de la Rance**, a hydro-electric station bridge which produces electricity by harnessing the tidal waters of the Rance. It is possible to have a guided tour of the Barrage. Dinard is a very fashionable holiday resort often nicknamed the Pearl of the Emerald Coast. It has beautiful sheltered beaches and picturesque coastal walks which were enjoyed by the British a hundred years ago. The main beach, the **Plage de l'Ecluse**, lies between the **Pointe du Moulinet** and the **Pointe de la Malouine**. Close by there is the casino and a miniature golf course. A walk to the Pointe du Moulinet gives the tourist a fine panorama of sea and rocks. Very close to Dinard is the elegant little resort of **Saint-Lunaire** with its two magnificent beaches, which are ideal for children to run about freely and explore the rock pools, and which are not as crowded as Dinard.

Just a few miles to the south of Dinard is the old town of **Dinan**, with its narrow streets, ancient houses, trees and gardens and its château and ramparts. It reminds the visitor very much of York and is well worth a visit, especially on market day (when it is unfortunately very difficult to park). The old town is famous for its fifteenth and sixteenth century shops with their wooden porches and triangular gable ends. The main part of the town is on a plateau which stands two hundred feet above the Rance. There is a good view of the river and the pleasure craft harbour from the **Jardin Anglais** (English Garden) behind the **Basilique Saint-Sauveur**. The castle keep is over a hundred feet high and dates from the fourteenth century. It now contains a museum of local history. There is also a fifteenth century clock tower called the **Tour de L'Horloge**. A visit to Dinan should be a priority.

On a day trip from Saint Malo going eastwards you could have a picnic lunch at the **Pointe du Grouin**, a rocky, wild piece of coastline with views as far as **Cap Fréhel** to the west and **Mont Saint Michel** to the east. Just off the Pointe is the **Ile des Landes**, an uninhabited island which is a natural sea bird reserve. Next you come to **Cancale**, centre of the oyster industry and a working port. It is not very picturesque but it is interesting to see the oyster beds at low tide and there are some good seafood restaurants. Try to call at **Dol-de-Bretagne**, a pleasant little market town on your way to **Le Vivier-sur-Mer** which is famous for its mussels. A few miles to the south east is **Fougères**, which has an interesting château whose massive walls and eleven large towers make it look formidable. You can walk all the way round the ramparts. Just to the west of Fougères and on the way back to Saint Malo is **Combourg**, which also has a picturesque château. On the third Sunday in May there is a flower and folklore festival.

Another day you might drive west from Saint Malo and visit **Saint-Cast**, which has a superb beach situated between the **Pointe de Saint-Cast** and the **Pointe de la Garde**. Then you should

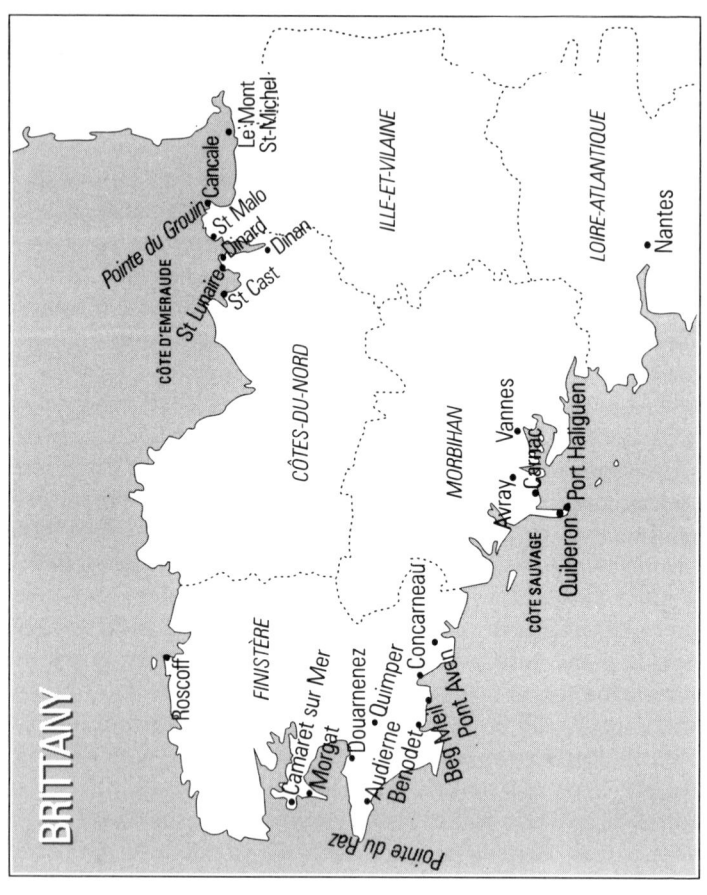

visit **Cap Fréhel**, one of the most impressive points in Brittany, with its high cliffs and magnificent panoramas of the **Pointe du Grouin** to the east and **Ile de Bréhat** in the west.

One type of holiday you might not have considered is canal cruising. From **Saint Malo** to **Redon** you can explore the Canal **D'Ille et Rance** and the river Vilaine and from there you could reach the **Canal de Nantes** and travel as far as **Josselin**.

Northern Brittany has lots to offer and for us is an ideal region to visit. The newcomer to France will find it rewarding and easy to negotiate.

♦ *South Brittany (Quimper and Carnac areas)*

This region, **Basse Bretagne** (Lower Brittany), stretches from **Camaret** (near Brest) down to **Vannes** and is made up of two *départements*: **Finistère** and **Morbihan**. Most of the interest is on the coast. There are two popular routes to this part of Brittany. If you take an overnight ferry from **Plymouth** to **Roscoff** you can then reach the area of **Quimper** in about two hours and the roads are usually very quiet. The other alternative is the **Portsmouth** to **Saint Malo** crossing which would allow you to reach the **Carnac** area in about three hours or so. Saint Malo to Quimper takes about four hours. There is no direct route but Saint Malo – Dinan – Lamballe – Quintin – Gourin – Quimper is probably the easiest.

This part of Brittany is full of tradition. It even still has its own ancient Celtic language which is related to those of Cornwall, Wales and Scotland. In fact the peninsula to the west of Quimper is known as 'la Cornouaille'. Many place names begin with the prefixes Tre, Pen or Lan as they do in Cornwall. It is thought that about a million people can speak Breton and in many towns and villages you can see evidence of the language on signs and shop windows.

The Breton people are very religious and there are a large number of calvaries and crosses, usually roughly made out of granite. One of the most memorable aspects of Breton life is the number of Pardons which take place annually. A Pardon is a religious procession usually led by the parish priest in which the villagers dress up in local costume and walk to a calvary or to the church in order to have their sins forgiven or to ask God for special favours. The wonderful thing about Pardons is that the local people make visitors feel welcome and you can join in the procession and the prayers. After the religious part there is usually a fête in a local meadow with lots of eating, drinking, dancing and singing. The music is very distinctive since it is played on ancient Breton instruments such as pipes, trumpets and bagpipes. Pardons are usually advertised in the villages and you can find out dates from the tourist offices. A visit to a Pardon is an experience of local colour not to be missed. For more information about traditional Breton festivals, write to the Fédération des Comités de Fêtes Folkloriques Bretonnes, 4, rue de la Ville Liard, 35800 Saint-Briac-sur-Mer.

Although most traditional costumes are only worn on special religious occasions it is also possible to see them every day, particularly in Quimper, Pont-Aven, Pont L'Abbé and Plougastel where some older women wear them all the time. The costume usually consists of simple black dresses with beautifully embroidered lace hats and pinafores. Anyone who is interested in costume will be able to buy postcards, books and dolls.

All over Brittany there are thousands of megaliths or large stones, some of which date back to five thousand years before Christ. Some of them, called **'menhirs'**, stand alone. Others are in alignments. Nobody really knows exactly why they were placed there or even how, because some of them weigh many tons. There are also **dolmens**, piles of stones which seem to have some funereal significance. There are more than three thousand menhirs and dolmens in the **Carnac** area alone.

As in North Brittany, seafood is very plentiful. *Homard* (lobster) is particularly popular cooked in the Breton style (*à l'Armoricaine*). Breton lamb with white haricot beans is a speciality as are partridge and hare. This is also the area for potatoes, artichokes, cauliflowers and peas. Other local specialities include the lace pancakes (*crêpes dentelles*) from Quimper, Breton galettes and biscuits from Nantes.

The only wine produced in Brittany is **Muscadet** which comes from the vineyards south of the Loire near Nantes. It is a light, dry wine ideal for drinking with seafood. There are three main types of Muscadet: Muscadet de Sèvre-et-Maine which is fine and light; Muscadet des Coteaux de la Loire which is drier and fruitier and Le Gros Plant which comes from Nantes and is light and pale. All Muscadet wine should be drunk chilled and young.

The most westerly part of south Brittany can be easily explored by using the typically Breton town of **Quimper** as a centre. Quimper, situated at the confluence of the rivers Steir and Odet is the regional capital of Finistère. It has a beautiful Gothic cathedral dating back to the thirteenth century, an old town with ancient houses, a museum of Breton culture which illustrates Breton history, archaeology, folklore, furniture, costumes and pottery and a pottery factory and workshops. Local traditional costume can be seen here on market days and more particularly at the great Festival of Cornouaille on the fourth Sunday in July. When you try to park in Quimper you will find it best to aim for the centre by driving towards the cathedral and then park down by the riverside which is close by. Try to avoid driving in and out during the rush hour. From Quimper you can sail down the river Odet past woods and châteaux park lands to **Bénodet**, **Loctudy** and the **Iles de Glénan**.

Thirty-five kilometres to the west of Quimper is the fishing port of **Audierne**, which has long sandy beaches with beach clubs for children. There is a daily boat service from here to the **Ile de Sein**. Very close to Audierne is the **Pointe du Raz**, a wild, windswept point very similar to Land's End in Cornwall with its rugged outcrops of rocks and lighthouses. On your way back from Audierne try to call at the small village of **Pont-Croix** to see its old streets. Just above Pont-Croix is the fishing port of **Douarnenez-Tréboul** where you can see mackerel, sardines, tuna and shellfish being landed. The town itself is not very attractive because of its canning factories and working port, but there are several beaches, an old quarter to visit and a shipping museum. Very close to Douarnenez is the splendid weavers' village of **Locronan**, which is a photographer's paradise. The heart of the village is a large square dominated by the fifteenth century priory church and graced by fourteenth, seventeenth and eighteenth century houses, many of which are shops. Narrow cobbled streets radiate from the square and reveal more old houses. There are some excellent craft shops to wander round and two or three good restaurants. Locronan was the setting for the Roman Polanski film *Tess* and has formed the background of more than twenty other films.

On another excursion from Quimper you could spend a very pleasant day exploring the **Crozon Peninsula**. Call first at the town of **Chateaulin** on the river Aulne. The river flows through the town in the form of a canal. It is a very pleasant spot for a picnic. The Crozon Peninsula is cross-shaped with the ocean surrounding it on all sides and filling hundreds of narrow creeks and indentations. The most frequented holiday resort is **Morgat**, which has a large, sheltered sandy beach. There is a small working port and a pleasure craft port. There is good sea-fishing in the area and there are some caves you can explore by boat. To the west of Crozon you will find the **Pointe de Penhir**, another dramatic 'Land's End', with its *tas de pois* (pile of peas), a group of rocks in the sea. You will also see a large monument which was erected to commemorate the heroic efforts of Bretons fighting with the free French during the last war. Finally, try to pay a short visit to **Camaret-sur-Mer**, a very quiet, picturesque little fishing port and holiday resort.

Just south of Quimper another small group of resorts will provide you with enjoyable visits. One of the most popular places to stay for English people is **Bénodet**, which is situated at the mouth of the Odet. It has everything for young families: a very safe sandy beach with life guards on duty; beach clubs and trampolines and lots of other amusements; a tree-lined promenade; fishing, tennis, sailing and boat trips on the river Odet to Quimper and across the sea to the **Iles de Gléhan**. Very close to Bénodet is **Beg-Meil**, whose excellent beach has a wealth of rock pools and a very pleasant cliff walk. Just across the small bay is **Concarneau**, one of the largest fishing ports in France. The main point of interest here, apart from the arrival of the fishing fleet, is the *Ville Close*, a small walled town surrounded by water. Its narrow streets are full of tourist shops, restaurants and *crêperies*. Its ramparts date back to the fourteenth century. At the entrance bridge there is an impressive clock tower. In the old arsenal there is a museum illustrating the history of Concarneau and the evolution of the fishing industry. Concarneau also has two beaches. While you are visiting Concarneau it would be worth making a slight detour to look at **Pont-Aven**. This little town is situated in a picturesque setting on the river Aven. Paul Gauguin, the artist, formed a painting school here and you can see why when you walk along the river to the *Bois d'Amour* (the Lovers' Wood).

If you go further south into the *département* of **Morbihan** there is another group of holiday resorts to enjoy. The best place to use as a centre is **Carnac**. In fact there are two Carnacs, Carnac town and Carnac-Plage, which are only a few hundred yards apart. The town has tree-lined avenues and shops and is a very pleasant shopping centre. **Carnac-Plage** is protected on its northern boundary by a wooded dune and in the east and west by the headlands of **Saint-Columban** and **Beaumer**. It has five beaches which slope gently into the sea and which are completely safe for bathing, even at high tide. Like Bénodet, Carnac is an ideal resort for families. There are beach games, tennis, riding, an eighteen hole golf course, mini-golf, yachting and a sailing school. There are cinemas, folklore festivals, dancing and the great Festival of the *Menhirs*. The long avenues of *menhirs* (standing stones) are known all over the world. The Ménec, Kermario and Kerlescan avenues extend over three to four kilometres and there are two thousand five hundred stones. There is an archaeological museum in Carnac with relics found in the Tumulus of Saint-Michel, a large burial mound just outside the town. Carnac is also well known for its Thalassotherapy Centre, where sea water and seaweed are used for medical treatment. Just next to Carnac the small town of **La Trinité-sur-Mer** has a good market.

From Carnac it is only a short distance to the **Quiberon Peninsula**. As you drive down to Quiberon the peninsula is so narrow that you can see the sea on both sides of the road. Quiberon has a fine sandy beach, a fishing port and a pleasure port at **Port-Haliguen**. The western side of the peninsula is called the **Côte Sauvage** (the Wild Coast). It is rich in cliffs, caves, crevices and small sandy beaches which are not too safe for bathing. The walks in the area are very good.

Just above the Golfe du Morbihan are the ancient towns of **Auray** and **Vannes**. Auray is on the river Loc whose wooded promenade affords a pretty view of the port and of the old district called Saint-Goustan, with its fifteenth century houses. Vannes is an important market town. Its picturesque old quarters are grouped round the cathedral and enclosed by fourteenth century ramparts. From either of these towns those who are interested in history can take the Route des Ducs de Bretagne and visit the *châteaux* of Suscino, Plessis-Josso, L'Estier, Lehélec, Rochefort-en-Terre, Largoët, Brignac, Le Crévy, Josselin and the Château de Rohan at Pontivy.

Finding Accommodation

The busiest month of the year in France is August and accommodation is difficult to find unless you have booked in advance. If your holiday dates are flexible you will find it a great advantage to go early, in May or June, or late, in September. It is much cheaper out of season, there are no crowds and the beaches are empty. Even outside peak holiday periods however it is wise to book in advance so that you have somewhere definite to make for at least on the first night. We well remember once travelling two hundred and fifty miles by car in France and then having to try eight campsites before finding a tiny space to put up our tent!

♦ *Camping*

If you have never camped before you may wish to try it out by having your holiday organised by a travel company which specialises in ready erected tents or luxury caravans. This can be a very enjoyable experience. The only slight disadvantage of this kind of holiday is that you tend to meet fewer French people because your campsite neighbours are usually English and you do not have much opportunity to practise your French. Why not try travelling independently and going to a 'French' site? There are thousands of campsites, from the very basic to the luxurious. The best campsite guide is called *Camping Caravaning France* published and revised annually by Michelin and is available at most good bookshops. Look for the familiar green coloured Michelin cover. Each site is graded for quality. Instead of stars they use tents, from one to five. We have always found that three tents is adequate and often very comfortable. Four tents is usually excellent. At the beginning of the guide all the symbols used are explained in English. You can find out the quality of the site, its address, the facilities offered, the approximate cost and whether it is possible to book in advance. (Some sites do not take advance reservations).

Most of the sites in the Michelin guide have washrooms and showers, good pitches for tents and caravans, a shop and a childrens' play area. Some have a supermarket and a café-restaurant. It depends on how much you want to pay and where the site is situated.

When you have chosen two or three suitable sites, you can easily obtain a brochure, an up to date price list and information about reservation. Try sending this letter.

YOUR FULL ADDRESS AND POSTCODE
(printed clearly)

Monsieur,

Veuillez m'envoyer, s'il vous plaît, votre brochure et votre tarif 199-.
Il est possible de réserver en avance?
Je vous prie d'agréer, Monsieur, mes sentiments distingués.

YOUR NAME (print).

Many campsites will send you information in English. Campsite charges are normally made per tent (or caravan), per person and per car. An extra charge is made for mains electricity. When you have chosen your campsite, write this letter to make a reservation. (To avoid errors with numbers and dates, use figures). These months may be useful – *mai* (May), *juin* (June), *juillet* (July), *août* (August), *septembre* (September).

YOUR FULL ADDRESS AND POSTCODE
(printed clearly)

Monsieur,

Je voudrais réserver une place à votre camping. C'est pour
___ tente(s), caravane(s)
___ adulte(s)
___ enfant(s) (children)

___ *voiture(s) (cars)*
___ *nuit(s) (nights)*
___ *branchement d'électricité (electrical hook-up)*
du (from the) 22 juin au (to the) 3 juillet (alter the date accordingly).
Je vous remercie et je vous prie d'agréer, Monsieur, mes sentiments distingués.

YOUR NAME (printed)

If the owner accepts your reservation he may mention in his reply the word *arrhes*. This refers to a deposit and means that your reservation is provisional and will be confirmed on receipt of a stated amount of deposit (usually twenty-five per cent of the total cost) within a reasonable amount of time. Sometimes a definite date is specified. This is normal procedure. The best way to send a deposit is to take this letter to your bank and ask for an international bank draft made payable in French francs to the proprietor of the site. Set out a letter as before with the following wording:

Monsieur,

Je vous envoie les arrhes que vous avez demandés. J'attends votre confirmation.
Je vous prie d'agréer, Monsieur, mes sentiments distingés.

Voilà! Your campsite is booked.

What to say on a campsite

I've reserved a place in the name of – J'ai réservé un emplacement au nom de . . .
Here is my letter of confirmation – Voici ma lettre de confirmation.
Have you got a vacant pitch? – Vous avez un emplacement de libre?
Have you any room left for tonight? – Vous avez encore de la place pour cette nuit?

I would like to stay for . . . nights – Je voudrais rester . . . nuits.

There are four of us – Nous sommes quatre.

It is for a tent, a caravan – C'est pour une tente, une caravane.

How much is it per person per night? – C'est combien par personne par nuit?

Is there an extra charge for a little (extra) tent, for an awning? – Il y a un supplément pour une petite tente, pour un auvent?

Where can I park the car? – Où est-ce que je peux garer la voiture?

I prefer a pitch in the shade, near the washing facilities – Je préfère un emplacement à l'ombre, près du bloc sanitaire.

I need an electrical hook-up – J'ai besoin d'un branchement d'électricité.

Are the showers free of charge? – Les douches sont gratuites?

Have you any ice? – Vous avez de la glace?

Is there a shop on the site, close by? – Il y a un magasin dans le camping, à proximité?

Are there any shops near here? – Il y a des commerces près d'ici?

Can we buy some milk, bread, camping gas? – Est-ce qu'on peut acheter du lait, du pain, du gaz butane?

Is the water drinking water? – L'eau est potable?

Where are the dustbins? – Où sont les poubelles?

Can we have a barbecue? – Est-ce qu'on peut faire un barbecue?

Have you any letters for me? – Vous avez des lettres pour moi?

Do you have take-away cooked meals? – Vous avez des plats cuisinés à emporter?

Do you have bikes for hire? – Vous avez des vélos à louer?

Do you have any leaflets about the region? – Vous avez des dépliants de la région?

Where is . . .? – Où est . . .?

   the sink for washing clothes – le bac à linge
   the washing up sink – le bac à vaisselle
   the washing facilities – le bloc sanitaire
   the reception office – le bureau d'accueil
   the drinking water – l'eau potable

the campsite warden – le gardien
the laundry – la laverie
the ironing room – la salle de repassage
the camping gas shop – le dépôt de butane

where are . . .? – ou sont . . .?

the showers – les douches
the childrens' play area – les jeux d'enfants
the dustbins – les poubelles

Other useful vocabulary to do with camping

Matches – Des allumettes, **Water carrier** – Un bidon
Electric torch – Une lampe de poche, **Camping gas** – Le camping gaz
Batteries – Des piles, **Sleeping bag** – Un sac de couchage
Electric point – Une prise de courant, **Lilo** – Un matelas pneumatique

♦ *Staying in a hotel*

If you wish to stay in a hotel in France in July or August it would be best to book in advance. You can obtain a list of hotels by writing to the local tourist office. Address your letter to Le Syndicat d'Initiative, Name of town, France. The letter should read as follows:

YOUR ADDRESS (printed)

Monsieur,

Veuillez m'envoyer, s'il vous plaît, une liste des hôtels dans votre ville.
Je vous prie d'agréer, Monsieur, mes sentiments distingués.

YOUR NAME (printed)

Alternatively, you could visit your local library and consult the red Michelin guide for France, which gives a comprehensive list

HOTEL DU STYVEL **

M. & Mme TEPHANY

Fruits de mer - Restaurant
29570 CAMARET - sur - MER
Tél. : 98 27 92 74

BAR L'OCÉAN

M. et Mme LE DOUARIN
* téléphone direct
* télévision dans chaque chambre
* salles de réunion
* chiens admis
* face au port, terrasse

4, place Gambetta **97.47.22.81**
Port de Vannes

BEL OMBRA ** NN

Hôtel-Pension de Famille

——— Au calme ———
600 m de la plage et Centre Ville
Rue des Maures - 83240 CAVALAIRE - Tél. 94.64.04.68

of hotels, together with details of the degree of comfort, the quality of the food, the facilities offered and prices.

There is an excellent organisation called the RELAIS ROUTIERS, which offers accommodation to lorry drivers, in the first place, but which welcomes tourists and provides accommodation at a very reasonable price. A list of these hotels is contained in the *Guide des Relais Routiers* which you can buy in your local bookshop or borrow from the library. If you have difficulty finding a copy write to Librairie Hachette, 4, Regent Place, London W1R 6BH. The symbols used in the guide are explained in English. One word of warning, however, some Routiers hotels are closed in August.

When you receive hotel information from a tourist office the following words may need translation:

Dates d'ouverture – **Dates of opening**

Chambres – **Bedrooms**

Douche – **Shower**

Salle de bains – **Bathroom**

Pension complète – **Full board**

Demi-pension – **Half board**

Repas – **Meals**

Petit déjeuner – **Breakfast**

Déjeuner – **Lunch**

Dîner – **Evening meal**

Prix – **Prices**

Prix tous compris – **Net price**

Ascenseur – **Lift**

Vue de mer – **Sea view**

Service compris – **Service included**

Service non compris – **Service not included**

When you book a hotel, the price you are quoted is normally for the room and not per person. In some hotels, especially *pensions de famille* you can book a family room which is usually good value for money. Normally, breakfast is not included in the price. It consists of croissants or bread with butter and jam and a large bowl of coffee. Some hotels do not serve meals at all. If you wish to eat in your hotel you should look for a *hôtel-restaurant* or a *pension* (which is more like a family run boarding house).

In order to make a hotel reservation by letter, put your address in the usual place and use a combination of the following phrases:

Dear Sir – Monsieur
I would like to reserve – Je voudrais réserver
A room with a single bed – Une chambre à un lit
A room with two beds – Une chambre à deux lits
A room with a double bed – Une chambre à un grand lit
There are four of us – Nous sommes quatre
For . . . people – Pour . . . personnes
With a shower, bathroom, toilet – Avec douche, salle de bains, toilette
It is for one, two, ten nights – C'est pour une, deux, dix nuits
From the (+ date) – A partir du
Until the (+date) – Jusqu'au

End the letter in the usual way. Here is a letter for your to imitate:

Monsieur,

Je voudrais réserver une chambre à deux lits pour deux personnes avec douche et toilette à partir du sept jusqu'au quatorze juillet, 199-.

Je vous prie d'agréer, Monsieur, mes sentiments distingués.

When you receive a reply, you may be expected to send a deposit. Follow the procedure set out for booking a campsite.

On arrival at a hotel you will be obliged to fill in a form called a *fiche de voyageur*, which is easy to understand because the headings are shown in English as well as French. This form asks for your personal details, plus information from your passport and your date of entry into France. Do not be surprised if you are asked to hand in your passport until you leave.

In your hotel room you will always find the price of the room, the rules and regulations of the hotel and possibly the times of meals displayed on the back of the door.

Expect to find some minor differences in a French hotel bedroom. Instead of a pillow you may find a long bolster. You will find shutters on the window which are designed to keep out various nuisances such as cold, wind, sunlight, flies and moths. You may find that the toilet has an unusual flush mechanism. You will probably not be able to remove the plug from the sink. It lifts up and down with a lever.

Campsites and hotels usually demand a *taxe de séjour*, which they are obliged by law to charge. It is a very small amount per person per day and will make little difference to the cost of your stay.

What to say in a hotel

Have you a vacant room? – Avez-vous une chambre de libre?
Can you recommend another hotel nearby? – Pouvez-vous me recommander un autre hôtel près d'ici?
I have reserved a room in the name of – J'ai réservé une chambre au nom de.
I would like two rooms for one night – Je voudrais deux chambres pour une nuit.
It is for one night only – C'est pour une nuit seulement.
I would like to stay for two days – Je voudrais rester deux jours.
A room for two people – Une chambre à deux personnes.
A room with a double bed – Une chambre à un grand lit.
A room with two beds – Une chambre à deux lits.
A room for one person – Une chambre à une personne.
A family room – Une chambre de famille.
A room with a shower – Une chambre avec douche.
A room with a bathroom – Une chambre avec salle de bain.
A room with a washbasin – Une chambre avec lavabo.
A room with a toilet – Une chambre avec cabinet de toilette.
A room with a balcony – Une chambre avec balcon.
A room with a sea view – Une chambre avec vue de mer.
What price is it? – C'est à quel prix?
How much is it per night? – C'est combien par nuit?
How much is half board? – C'est combien avec demi-pension?
How much is full board? – C'est combien avec pension complète?
What floor is it on? – C'est à quel étage?
May I see the room? – Je peux voir la chambre?

It's exactly what we need – C'est exactement ce qu'il nous faut.
It's not really what we are looking for – Ce n'est pas tout à fait ce qu'il nous faut.
I'm sorry, it's a bit too expensive – Je regrette, c'est un peu trop cher.
I'll take it – Je la prends.
Is the breakfast included? – Le petit déjeuner est compris?
What time is breakfast? – Le petit déjeuner est à quelle heure?
What time is the evening meal? – Le dîner est à quelle heure?
Is there a restaurant, a car park, a lift in the hotel? – Il y a un restaurant, un parking, un ascenseur dans l'hôtel?
What time does the hotel close in the evening? – L'hôtel ferme à quelle heure le soir?
I'm going to be back late tonight – Je vais rentrer tard ce soir.
Do I need a key for the front door? – Il me faut une clé pour la porte d'entrée?
Give me a key for room number — – Donnez-moi la clé de la chambre —.
Are there any letters for me? – Il y a des lettres pour moi?
Is my bill ready? – Vous avez préparé ma note?
I would like my bill please – Je voudrais ma note, s'il vous plaît.
Do you accept cheques? – Vous acceptez des chèques?
I will be leaving tomorrow – Je partirai demain.

Complaints

I would like another blanket – Je voudrais bien une autre couverture.
The lift is not working – L'ascenseur ne marche pas.
The room is dirty – Le chambre est sale.
There is no soap/towel in the room – Il n'y a pas de savon/serviette dans la chambre.
I can't turn the tap off – Je n'arrive pas à fermer le robinet.

♦ *Staying at a Gîte*

What is a *gîte*? It may be a small cottage, a village house, a converted flat in the owner's house or part of a farm building. *Gîtes* are usually situated in or near small country villages, occasionally within reach of the sea. The accommodation is simple but adequate and often in a picturesque setting. *Gîtes* offer very good value for money. The owners are country people who enjoy having visitors and they often live on the premises or in the vicinity, which can be very convenient if your gas bottle needs changing! The owners do not normally speak English but part of the fun of this type of holiday is trying to communicate with the locals. The houses are away from holiday resorts and they offer a peaceful retreat where you can enjoy the delights of rural France.

The French Tourist Office in London can supply you with a list of dozens of companies which have villas and houses for rent and which will also make your travel arrangements. If you have never visited France this can be a convenient way of booking accommodation. Everything is done for you but, of course, you pay for the service. Alternatively you can obtain the addresses of all the local offices of the National Federation of *Gîtes* in France from the London office.

Most people do not realise that as well as relying on villa rental companies you can book a *gîte* directly, either through the local tourist office of the region or through the owner. Not only is it cheaper but there is a great deal of satisfaction to be gained from doing it yourself. Write to the tourist office in your chosen area of France as follows:

YOUR ADDRESS (print)

Monsieur,

Voudriez-vous m'envoyer, s'il vous plaît, votre brochure 'Gîtes de France'.
Je vous prie d'agréer, Monsieur, mes sentiments distingués.

YOUR NAME (print)

N° 92 · 3 épis* NN · 4/6 p. · SUSSEY

« Au bourg » à 15 km de SAULIEU. Maison mitoyenne. R.-C.
Séjour-cuisine avec cheminée en service et 1 convertible.
2 chambres : 1 lit 2 pl., 2 lits 1 pl. Salle de bains. Chauffage
électrique et au bois. Draps et linge de maison fournis. Poss.
loc. bicyclettes. Salle de jeux au 1er étage. Lave-linge. TV.
Cour fermée. Garage.
Lac Chamboux 12 km : pêche, voile. Piscine, cheval 15 km.
Baignade 7 km.
Propriétaire : GARREAU Marie-Paule, SUSSEY, 21430 LIER-
NAIS, tél. 80.84.40.47.

Carte : B4

H. SAISON	V. SCOL.	JUIN/SEPT.	JUIL./AOUT	W.E.
1 000 F	1 200 F	1 200 F	1 350 F	600 F

N° 209 · 3 épis NN · 6/9 p. · SUSSEY

« Au Bourg » à 8 km de LIERNAIS. Maison mitoyenne. R.-C.
et 1er étage. Cuisine-séjour avec cheminée et con-
vertible. 3 chambres : 2 lits 1 pl., 2 lits 2 pl., 2 lits enf. 1 salle
de bains et 1 salle d'eau. Radiateurs électriques. Lave-linge.
TV. Possibilité location bicyclettes et draps. Terrasse.
Lac, pêche, tennis, équitation 15 km. Baignade 7 km.
Propriétaire : GARREAU Marie-Paule, SUSSEY, 21430 LIER-
NAIS, tél. 80.84.40.47.

Carte : B4

H. SAISON	V. SCOL.	JUIN/SEPT.	JUIL./AOUT	W.E.
1 200 F	1 300 F	1 300 F	1 450 F	700 F

N° 246 · EC · 6 p. · SUSSEY

« Vouvres » à 4 km, à 12 km de SAULIEU. Maison indépendante. R.-C. et 2 étages. Cuisine. Séjour avec cheminée.
3 chambres : 1 lit 2 pl., 4 lits 1 pl. Salle d'eau. Chauffage électrique. Prise TV. Jardin clos. Portique. ✿
Forêt, chasse sur place. Etang, plage, pêche 15 km. Piscine
découverte, tennis, équitation 12 km.
▓▓▓▓▓▓▓ : 80.50.15.60.

Carte : B4

H. SAISON	V. SCOL.	JUIN/SEPT.	JUIL./AOUT	W.E.
1 150 F	1 380 F	1 150 F	1 380 F	650 F

N° 150 · 3 épis · 5 p. · VENAREY-LES-LAUMES

« Au bourg ». Maison mitoyenne dans un ensemble de bâtiments. R.-C. cuisine. 1 séjour avec convertible. 1 chambre :
1 lit 2 pl. 1 chambrette 1 lit 1 pl. 1 salle d'eau. Chauffage électrique. Poss. loc. draps. TV. Petite cour intérieure.
Pêche, tennis, plan d'eau sur place. ✿
Propriétaire : MURGEY Alice, 14, rue Bouhey-Allex, 21150
VENAREY-LES-LAUMES, tél. 80.96.01.40.

Carte : B3

H. SAISON	V. SCOL.	JUIN/SEPT.	JUIL./AOUT	W.E.	
750 F	750 F	800 F	900 F	500 F	930 F

The brochure will contain a booking form, a map of the region showing the location of all the *gîtes* advertised and a list of illustrated properties which can be hired through the owner. If you do not know much French it is probably easier to book through the tourist office, where there is usually someone who speaks English.

The addresses shown below cover most of Normandy and Brittany and provide a selection of hundreds of *gîtes*. Write to the 'syndicat d'initiative' (office de tourisme) of the largest town in the area you want.

Calvados (Normandy) – Relais Départemental des Gîtes, 4, Promenade Madame de Sévigné, 14039 Caen.
Manche (Normandy) – Relais Départemental des Gîtes, Préfecture, 50009 Saint Lô.
Ille et Vilaine (Brittany) – Relais Départemental des Gîtes, 1, rue Martenot, 35000 Rennes.
Côtes du Nord (Brittany) – Association des Gîtes Ruraux, 28, boulevard Hérault, BP 556, 22010 Saint Brieuc.

Some useful phrases

When you receive your brochure it will be in French, but the words and phrases used are easy to follow with the aid of the following list.

Types of Gîte

Gîtes are classified by 'épis' (ears of corn): one épi is a gîte with basic comfort; two épis denotes a good standard of comfort; three épis is very comfortable.

Maison indépendente – **A detached property**
Gîte dans la même maison que le logement du propriétaire – **A gîte situated in the same building as the owner**.
Gîte situé sur l'exploitation agricole/gîte à la ferme – **A gîte situated on a farm**.

Gîte situé dans un ensemble de bâtiments – **A gîte situated within a group of buildings.**
Gîte situé à l'étage d'une maison – **A gîte situated on the upper floor of a house.**
Gîte situé au rez de chaussée – **A gîte situated on the ground floor.**
Ancienne ferme rénovée – **An old renovated farm.**
Bâtiment rénové – **A renovated building.**

Facilities offered

Le gîte comprend – **The gîte includes,** Entrée indépendente – **Separate entrance**
Salle de séjour – **Living room,** Cuisine – **Kitchen**
Salle de bains – **Bathroom,** Salle d'eau – **Bathroom, shower room**
Studio – **Bed sitting-room,** Salle commune avec coin cuisine – **Living room with corner kitchen**
Chambre – **Bedroom,** Chambre palière – **Bedroom on Landing**
Lit d'enfant – **Child's bed,** Lit de bébé – **Baby's cot**
Lit une place – **Single bed,** Lit deux places – **Double bed**
Divan convertible – **Bed settee,** Canapé lit – **Bed settee**
Fauteuil lit – **Bed settee,** Lit pliant – **Folding bed**
Chauffage central – **Central heating,** par convecteurs – **convector heaters,** à accumulation – **storage heaters,** au mazout – **oil fired heating,** au gaz – **gas heating,** électrique – **electric heating**
Eau chaude – **Hot water,** Poêle à charbon – **Coal stove**
Poêle à bois – **Wood stove,** Cuisinière – **Cooker**
Cheminée – **Fireplace,** Cellier – **Cellar**
Jardin clos – **Enclosed garden,** Pelouse – **Lawn**
Dépendances – **Outbuildings,** Terrain attenant – **Land attached**
Terrasse – **Patio,** Balcon – **Balcony**
Cour (close) – **Yard (enclosed),** Abri couvert (pour voiture) – **Shed (for car)**

Local recreational activities (pour vos loisirs)

A proximité – **Nearby,** Dans les environs – **In the vicinity**

Sur place – **On the spot**, Pêche – **Fishing**
Equitation – **Horse riding**, Piscine – **Swimming pool**
Forêt – **Forest**, Plage – **Beach**
Mer – **Sea**, Baignade – **Bathing**
Etang – **Pond or small lake**, Plan d'eau – **Stretch of water**
Petit bois privé – **Small private wood**, Promenades – **Walks**
Chasse – **Hunting**, Sentiers de grande randonnée – **Country paths for walking**

Other useful phrases

Nom du propriétaire – **Owner's name**, Hors saison – **Out of season**, Ouvert toute l'année – **Open all the year round**, Tarifs/prix de location pour une semaine – **Cost of hire per week**

The next step is to look in the brochure for two or three suitable *gîtes*. You will find a 'Fîche de Demande de Réservation' or a 'Bulletin de Réservation' (a booking form) which you should complete, putting the gîtes in order of preference. You will be asked for these details:

Nom – **Surname**, Prénoms – **First names**
Adresse – **Address**, Pays – **Country**
Adultes/enfants – **Adults/children**, Nombre de personnes – **Number of people**
Gîtes choisis par ordre de préférence – **Gîtes listed in order of preference**, Séjour souhaité – **Dates required**
Du samedi (date) . . . au samedi (date) – **From Saturday (date) . . . to Saturday (date)**.

The form should then be sent to the tourist office together with enough international reply coupons (Coupons Réponses) to cover postage. These are obtainable from the post office.

When you are offered a *gîte* you will receive two copies of a contract (*Un Contrat de Location*), which may well be in English. If it is in French you child's French teacher may offer to help you to fill it in. Keep on good terms with him! You have to fill in your part of the contract, sign and date it and send one copy back to France together with a twenty-five per cent deposit, which you obtain by going to your bank with the contract and asking for an international bank draft in French francs. The contract will make it clear to whom the draft is payable.

Your contract will contain a set of regulations which are both sensible and reasonable. They warn that damage must be paid for, that only the pre-arranged number of people should occupy the *gîte*, that blankets are included in the price but not sheets and towels and that the cost of heating is extra. There are other regulations including the fact that the owner has the right to re-let the property if you fail to arrive within two days of the hire date, and other minor points which are intended to safeguard the owner's interests. You may be asked to pay an extra returnable deposit to cover damage or breakages.

When you arrive in France to occupy your *gîte* you will be asked to pick up the keys either at the tourist office, whose address and location you will be given or at the property itself. You will be expected to pay the balance of your rental charge on arrival.

Staying in a *gîte* in France provides a real look at French life and an opportunity to meet French people. Trying to communicate with them is part of the fun of the holiday. Incidentally, if you are able to avoid July and August you will find numerous *gîtes* available at very reasonable prices.

The writer recommends this type of holiday.

What to say to a gîte owner

I am very pleased to meet you – Je suis très heureux de faire votre connaissance.
Excuse us for being late – Excusez-nous d'être en retard.
We got lost – Nous nous sommes perdus.
The ferry arrived late – Le ferry est arrivé en retard.
Here is my contract – Voici mon contrat de location.
Have you got the key? – Vous avez la clé?
Are there any shops nearby? – Il y a des magasins tout près?
Where can I buy some eggs, milk, bread? – Où est-ce que je peux acheter des oeufs, du lait, du pain?

Have you any milk? – Avez-vous du lait?
We have a problem. Come and see – Nous avons un problème. Venez voir.
I have broken a glass – J'ai cassé un verre.
There is no gas left – Il n'y a plus de gaz.
We have had a power cut/the electricity has gone off – Il y a une panne d'électricité.
We have no water – Nous n'avons plus d'eau.
The kitchen is dirty. Can you clean it? – La cuisine est sale. Pouvez-vous la nettoyer?
Have you any blankets? – Avez-vous des couvertures?
Have you any wood for the fire? – Avez-vous du bois pour le feu?
See you later – A tout à l'heure.
Would you like to have an aperitif with us? – Voudriez-vous boire un apéritif avec nous?
We have had an excellent stay – Notre séjour a été excellent.
I would like to thank you – Je voudrais vous remercier.
We would like to come back next year – Nous voudrions revenir l'année prochaine.
See you soon, I hope – A bientôt, j'espère.

◆ *Staying at a Youth Hostel*

Before you stay at a French hostel you need to join the Youth Hostels Association and obtain an international card which contains your photograph. You can write for information to the Fédération Unie des Auberges de Jeunesse, 6, rue Mesnil, 75116 Paris. Their brochure includes a map showing the situation and addresses of hostels, opening times, nearest towns, rail and bus stations, the number of beds available, the cost of accommodation, meals and hire of sheets and sleeping bags, facilities for cooking, a list of activities organised by the hostel and local tourist attractions. The F.U.A.J. is a non-profit making organisation whose aim is to help young people to travel the world, to take part in the many different activities organised by hostels and to meet other young people from other countries and different backgrounds.

Couples and families are welcomed at many hostels. You are recommended to contact hostels in advance to check whether they have room. Normally it is individual travellers and groups who are catered for. There is almost always room for casual travellers who turn up without a reservation. In many holiday areas you will also find *Centres d'Accueil*, which are very similar to youth hostels. They too offer reasonably priced accommodation. Addresses can be found in tourist brochures. In our experience they represent very good value for money.

What to say at a Youth Hostel

Is there a youth hostel nearby? – Il y a une auberge de jeunesse près d'ici?

I'm looking for the youth hostel – Je cherche l'auberge de jeunesse.

Where is the warden? – Où est le père aubergiste?

Have you any room left? – Vous avez encore de la place?

Have you a bed? – Vous avez un lit de libre?

Have you got two beds for tonight? – Il y a deux lits pour cette nuit?

It's for one night – C'est pour une nuit.

How much is it per day? – C'est combien par jour?

Can I hire some sheets/a sleeping bag? – Je peux louer des draps/un sac de couchage?

Where are the dormitories? – Où sont les dortoirs?

Where is the kitchen? – Où est la cuisine?

Can I do some cooking? – Je peux faire la cuisine?

Where do we have breakfast? – Où est-ce qu'on prend le petit déjeuner?

Where can I leave my bike/car? – Où est-ce que je peux laisser ma bicyclette/voiture?

The Exchange Visit

This section contains a few tips for the rare, fortunate tourist who is invited to spend some time in a French home, but it is mainly intended to help school children and students who have plucked up the courage to go on an exchange. Staying with a French family can be a wonderful experience and one which all students of French should have the opportunity to try. Practising your French whilst experiencing the real culture of the country is much more exciting than learning in a classroom. It also keeps you motivated to continue enjoying the language long after the visit is over. During your stay you may well make friends who will last a lifetime.

♦ *How to get the Best out of your Exchange Visit*

The whole experience of going to stay with a family is a public relations exercise. You have been invited into their home and everything you do and say matters a great deal. You are not only representing your own family and reflecting the way you have been brought up, you are also representing your school and your country. All English people will be judged, in the eyes of the family, by how *you* behave! A frightening thought?

Start off on the right track. A few days before you set off send a brief letter to your penfriend saying how much you are looking forward to going and write a few words thanking his or her parents in advance for having you. Use this letter as a starting point but try to add a few words of your own as well, even if they are in English.

YOUR ADDRESS
DATE

Cher Pierre,
(Chère Anne),

J'attends avec impatience ma visite chez vous – **I am looking forward very much to my visit to your house.**
J'arriverai chez vous (le trois juillet) – **I will arrive at your house on the (3rd July).**
Dis bonjour à tes parents – **Say hello to your parents for me.**
Je voudrais remercier tes parents pour m'avoir invité(e) – **I would like to thank your parents for inviting me.**
A bientôt – **See you soon.** *Cordialement* – **Yours sincerely.**

SIGNATURE

Next ask your parents to write a short letter to your penfriend's parents to give them when you arrive. Not only is this a nice gesture but it will also be an ice breaker and a talking point, especially if you have to tell them what it means in French! Some photographs of your family will also help you to begin to communicate without too much difficulty. Think carefully about a small present to take with you, possibly something typically English. We always used to take a box of After Eight mints before they became available in France. Whatever you come up with it will be appreciated.

Once you have arrived in France you need to be aware of a big difference in the way of life. The French are extremely polite people and it is very important that you try to conform to their ways. If you do not you will be considered to be bad mannered and stand-offish. It is normal to address male adults as *monsieur* and married ladies as *madame*. Use these words FREQUENTLY, particularly when you are saying *bonjour* and *au revoir*. Young ladies are usually addressed as *mademoiselle* but be careful not to address an older lady in that way, because it could be considered to be rude. If you are in doubt about a lady's age or about whether she is married address her as *madame*.

As you are probably aware from your French lessons there is a formal and an informal word for 'you'. You should address all adults as *vous* and children, friends and pets as *tu*. Yes, pets! Remember that they only respond to you when you talk to them in French!

Daily greetings are also very different. You will do lots of kissing, whether you like it or not! You will kiss all the female members of the family at least twice a day. Girls will kiss boys and boys will shake hands with the men and boys. It varies from region to region and family to family as to how many cheeks you kiss and in which order. The best strategy is to let the family take the lead and you just enjoy the experience! You will find that French people demonstrate their feelings much more than the English, who tend to be reserved and unwilling to make physical contact. You do get used to it though and once you have overcome your shyness it is a pleasant custom.

An exchange parent's biggest worry is that their guest is not enjoying the holiday. It has been known for some young people to stay in their room, refuse to eat anything and not say a word. French people are very sociable and talkative so do try not to clam up. Join in as best you can and continually look for things to say, particularly if you can compliment the mother about the food, the house, your room and the garden. You will find that at first you will not understand much of the French you are hearing. You will have to ask people to repeat things and talk more slowly. You will sometimes even stop trying to understand because your brain cannot cope with the volume of French around you. Persevere, it gets better! By the end of the stay you will have much more confidence and you will wonder what all the worry was about. Remember that the family will be very tolerant and sympathetic when you try to speak. The best people to practise on are toddlers. Their French is probably about the same level as yours! Go out of your way to ask them their name, their age, their likes and dislikes and what they are doing. Listening to young children speaking French is a joy.

There are many ways in which you can show consideration to a French family as well as trying your best to communicate with them. You need to demonstrate that you are happy by joining in the activities they have planned for you and by being as outgoing as possible, even if they are things you would not normally like doing. Do not sit glued to the television. Take every opportunity to offer to help in the kitchen, pack the car up for a day out or carry things about. Do not leave dirty clothes (or any clothes for that matter) lying in your room. Take a bin liner with you and put them in. Better still, hand wash them yourself! Do not lie in bed till lunchtime. Make your bed every morning, even if you do not do it at home. Keep your room tidy. Never say that anything is better in England. Accept their invitation to telephone your parents when you arrive, but then buy a telephone card and ring them from town. They will not appreciate you running up a large bill. If you find that you are running short of currency ask in good time to go to the bank to change your travellers' cheques so that they do not have to lend you any money. Take some extra money with you, not to spend, but just in case you run short. When they take you out offer to pay for yourself. They will refuse but the offer will be appreciated. You can pay them back in part by insisting on buying everybody an ice cream or a coffee. If ever you do not feel well tell someone before the symptoms develop too much. If you are on some kind of medication make sure that you take enough to last until you arrive home. The family would have great difficulty trying to explain to the chemist or doctor what you needed because the brand names are different. Take your E111 with you in case you need any medical treatment. Remember that the family is responsible for you while you are in their care. It would be very inconsiderate to make arrangments to go out with someone else or to go anywhere without telling them.

The time that you are most on show is at the dining table. Quite often before the meal the family will have *apéritifs*. These drinks can be very strong and on an empty stomach can make you feel very drunk. When I was twelve years old, on the first night of my exchange, my penfriend's father plied me with his home made cider, which I happily drank. I spent the whole night clutching the bed with my eyes open, because every time I closed them the bedroom spun round like a spinning top! Many French children dilute wine with mineral water. Many do not drink wine at all. By all means try it but in moderation. Some French fathers are so insistent on filling up your glass that they still carry on pouring when you put your hand over it!

At the table you have to be careful not to upset your hostess. She will be proud of what she has prepared and will feel deflated if you turn your nose up at it or will not try it. If you think you are not going to like something ask for a very small portion *un tout petit peu*. Always say please and thank you. If you definitely do not like something say so politely but try to eat everything else. Do not make the fatal mistake of filling up on the *hors d'oeuvres* (first course). There may be several more courses to come! It often helps that large meals especially at weekends are interspersed with long pauses during which the family chatter. Try to pace yourself so that you do not miss out on the desserts. One aspect of the meal which you may not like is the coffee. It is served black and quite strong. Say that you would prefer a soft drink. You will probably find that during the day you will rarely be offered a hot drink. If you like tea it might be sensible to take a few teabags with you. The worst cup of tea I have ever had in my life was when my hostess put some loose tea in a saucepan full of cold water and boiled it for about ten minutes! Teach them how to make a good cup of tea. It will be a talking point.

Breakfast is interesting. You may be offered hot chocolate or ground or instant coffee with hot milk in a large cup or a bowl with some bread, butter and jam. Do not be surprised to see people dunking their bread in their drink. Warm croissants are lovely especially on a Sunday morning. You are much less likely to be offered cereals and very unlikely to be given a cooked breakfast.

Be prepared for mealtimes to be different from yours. French children often have a snack at teatime (*le goûter*) because the evening meal can be at any time between seven and nine o'clock. You can imagine how hungry you will be if you have nothing to eat between lunchtime and eight or nine o'clock.

Just one final observation about eating with a French family. Watch and learn about their table customs and imitate them. Eating with the family could turn out to be one of the highlights of your visit.

Elsewhere in the house beware of the bathroom tap with 'C' on it. This is the hot tap. Do not confuse the bidet with the toilet. The bidet is for washing parts you cannot get into the sink! Except, that is, in a family I know where it is filled with water and the dog drinks out of it! Remember that electricity costs money. Do not spend ages in the shower. Expect to use a flannel glove (*un gant de toilette*) to wash with. In your bedroom you may well have a sausage shaped bolster instead of a pillow. There will probably be shutters on the windows, which keep out rain, wind, cold and insects. If you are in the country close your shutters before you put on the bedroom light unless you are very fond of moths! You can open them again when you have put out the light.

One final warning. Exercise extreme caution if you are invited to ride on the family's mobylette. They may not be as powerful as a motor bike but fourteen year olds ride them, sometimes without helmets, often with fatal results.

I have found staying with French families to be an unforgettable experience and one which is very much worth the effort.

When you arrive back in England do send a letter of thanks. These people have gone to a lot of trouble to accommodate and entertain you. The least you can do is to show your gratitude. Use this short note as the basis for your letter and show off the French you learned by adding some of your own ideas:

YOUR ADDRESS
DATE

Chers Monsieur et Madame

Je suis bien arrivé(e) chez moi – **I have arrived home safely**.
Je vous remercie beaucoup de mon séjour chez vous – **I would like to thank you very much for my stay at your house**.
Vous avez été très gentils – **You have been very kind**.
Je me suis très bien amusé(e) – **I have enjoyed myself very much**.
J'espère vous revoir bientôt – **I hope to see you again soon**.
Merci encore – **Thanks again**.
Cordialement – **Yours sincerely**.

SIGNATURE

Sooner or later the exchange partner will come to stay with you. Ask your parents to bear a few things in mind. You partner is coming to experience life in Britain. They should not try to prepare French meals but the ones you usually have. Your normal daily routine other than meals should be adhered to and there may be times when they may need to be firm about bedtimes and staying out late. Ask your parents not to be over-enthusiastic about talking all the time. Your friend will need some space and will become exhausted if expected to listen and speak incessantly. To avoid long silences on the other hand find things to do. Having said that, though, the partner is in Britain to learn English. No matter how good at speaking French you and your parents are, speak in English and allow your friend to do so as much as possible.

What to say to your Exchange Family

Many of the everyday phrases you will need to talk to the family are listed in the section about making initial contact and every day social language. Do try to learn as many of them as you can before you go to France. The following phrases may help your stay to run a little more smoothly.

When you first arrive

Excusez-noi, je ne comprends pas très bien – **I am sorry but I can't understand very well**.
Pouvez-vous répéter? – **Can you repeat it?**
Voulez-vous parler plus lentement? – **Will you speak more slowly?**
Voici un petit cadeau pour vous – **Here is a small gift for you**.
Enchanté, monsieur/madame – **I am very pleased to meet you**.
Je peux téléphoner à mes parents? – **May I telephone my parents?**
Je peux vous aider? – **Can I help you?**

Compliments

J'ai passé une merveilleuse journée (soirée) – **I have had a marvellous day (evening)**.

Tout le monde est très gentil – **Everyone is very kind.**
C'est très gentil, merci – **That's very kind, thank you.**
Je m'amuse très bien ici – **I am having a really good time here.**
Ça me plaît beaucoup – **I like it very much.**
C'est formidable! (chouette!) – **It's great!**
J'ai bien dormi, merci – **I have slept well, thank you.**

Problems

Je regrette un peu ma maison – **I am feeling a little bit home-
sick.**
Je ne me sens pas très bien – **I do not feel very well.**
Je n'ai pas de (dentifrice) – **I have no (toothpaste).**
Pourriez-vous me prêter . . .? – **Could you lend me . . .?**
Je peux avoir du papier hygénique? – **Can I have some toilet
paper?**
Je peux avoir une autre couverture (un oreiller)? – **Can I have
another blanket (a pillow)?**
Je peux prendre une douche (un bain)? – **Can I have a shower
(a bath)?**
Je peux me laver les mains? – **Can I wash my hands?**
Je peux laver mes vêtements? – **Can I wash my clothes?**
Je peux emprunter (un réveil-matin)? – **Can I borrow (an alarm
clock)?**

At the table

Bon appétit – **Enjoy your meal.** (Say this back to the family
when they have first said it to you.)
A votre santé! – **Your good health!**
J'ai très faim (soif) – **I am very hungry (thirsty).**
Où est-ce que je dois m'asseoir? – **Where do you want me to
sit?**
Un (tout) petit peu, s'il vous plaît – **A (tiny) little bit, please.**
Oui, je veux bien – **I would love some.**
Je regrette, mais je n'aime pas . . . – **I am sorry, but I do not
like . . .**

Merci – **Thank you** (if you say 'merci' before you have received the food it means 'no thank you').

C'est délicieux – **It is delicious.**

Avez-vous une fourchette, un couteau, un cuiller, un verre? – **Have you a fork, knife, spoon, glass?**

Pouvez-vous passer le pain, le sucre, le sel, le poivre, l'eau, le vin, le lait? – **Can you pass the bread, sugar, salt, pepper, water, wine, milk?**

Je peux prendre encore du potage, de la viande, des légumes, du pain? – **Can I have some more soup, meat, vegetables, bread?**

Merci, ça me suffit – **Thank you, I have enough.**

J'en ai assez mangé – **I have had enough to eat.**

J'ai très bien mangé, merci – **I have enjoyed my meal very much, thank you.**

Je peux quitter la table, s'il vous plaît? – **May I leave the table, please?**

Je peux vous aider à faire la vaisselle? – **May I help with the washing up?**

Leaving

Merci pour tout – **Thank you for everything.**

Merci encore – **Thank you again.**

J'ai passé des vacances merveilleuses – **I have had a wonderful holiday.**

Merci de votre hospitalité – **Thank you for your hospitality.**

A l'année prochaine (j'espère) – **See you next year (I hope).**

Everyday Social Language

French people, like other nationalities, do not like foreigners who refuse to try to speak their language. They appreciate our efforts to communicate in French, no matter how badly we do it. It is worth 'having a go' even if you feel that you are making a fool of yourself. English people have often said to us that when they have tried to communicate, they have been unable to express successfully even their most simple thoughts, requests and thanks. Hopefully, the following phrases will at least help you to make a start:

Hello and Goodbye

Hello – Bonjour

Good night – Bonne nuit

Hello (on telephone) – Allô

Goodbye – Au revoir

See you later – A tout à l'heure

See you tomorrow – A demain

Till the next time – A la prochaine fois

Good Evening – Bonsoir

Hi! – Salut

Here we are – Nous voici

See you soon – A bientôt

See you this evening – A ce soir

I'll leave you – Je vous laisse

See you next year – A l'année prochaine

Introductions

I am called – Je m'appelle
What are you called? – Comment vous appelez-vous?

What is your wife/husband called? – Comment s'appelle votre femme/mari?

What is your first name? – Quel est votre prénom?

I'd like to introduce you to my wife/husband/son/daughter – Je vous présente ma femme/mon mari/mon fils/ma fille.

This is Peter – Voici Peter.

Pleased to meet you – Enchanté.

Pleased to make your acquaintance – Heureux de faire votre connaissance.

I am English – Je suis Anglais(e)

Where do you come from? – D'où venez-vous?

How old are you? – Quel âge avez-vous?

I am . . . years old – J'ai . . . ans.

Have you been here long? – Vous êtes ici depuis longtemps?

What do you do for a living? – Que faites-vous dans la vie?

Sit down – Asseyez-vous.

How are you?

How are you? – Comment ça va?

How are you going on? – Comment allez-vous?

Very well thank you – Très bien, merci.

I am very well – Je vais très bien.

Please and Thank You

Please – S'il vous plaît.

Thank you (very much) – Merci (bien/beaucoup).

Thank you for your hospitality – Je vous remercie de votre hospitalité.

I thank you sincerely – Je vous remercie sincèrement.

Thank you for everything – Merci pour tout.

You are very kind – Vous êtes très gentil.

That's most kind – C'est très aimable.

You have been really nice – Vous avez été très sympa.

Not at all – De rien.

Don't mention it – Je vous en prie.

It's quite all right – Il n'y a pas de quoi.

We have spent a marvellous evening – Nous avons passé une soirée excellente
That meal was really delicious – Ce repas était vraiment délicieux.

Have a Nice Day!

Have a nice day – Bonne journée.
Have a nice evening – Bonne soirée.
Have a pleasant stay – Bon séjour.
Have a good holiday – Bonnes vacances.
Enjoy the rest of your holiday – Bonne fin de vacances.
Have a safe journey home – Bon retour.
Have a good journey – Bonne route.
Have a good trip – Bon voyage.
Enjoy your meal – Bon appétit.
Your very good health/cheers! – A votre santé.
Happy birthday – Bon anniversaire.
Merry Christmas – Joyeux Noël.
Happy new year – Bonne année.

I Beg your Pardon!

I do not understand – Je ne comprends pas.
What does that mean? – Qu'est-ce que cela veut dire?
Sorry! – Pardon!
What (did you say)? – Comment?
Excuse me, pardon me – Excusez-moi, je m'excuse.
I am very sorry – Je suis désolé.
I'm sorry – Je regrette.
Can you help me? – Pouvez-vous m'aider.
Repeat please – Répétez, s'il vous plaît.
Will you speak more slowly? – Voulez-vous parler plus lentement?
Do you speak English? – Vous parlez anglais?
Am I disturbing you? – Je vous dérange?
It's not serious – Ce n'est pas grave.
Don't worry about it – Ne vous en faites pas.

I am late – Je suis en retard.

Invitations, Accepting and Refusing

Would you like to dine with us? – Voulez-vous dîner avec nous?
Would you like to have an aperitif with us? – Vous voudriez prendre un apéritif avec nous?
Do you want to come with us? – Vous voulez venir avec nous?
What are you doing this evening? – Que faites -vous ce soir?
Are you free this evening? – Vous êtes libre ce soir?
Shall we go? – On y va?
I am inviting you (to dinner) – Je vous invite (à dîner).
What time shall we meet? – A quelle heure est-ce qu'on se rencontre?
Where shall we meet? – On se rencontre où?
Shall we telephone each other? – On se téléphone?
I'll see you later – Je vous verrai plus tard.
I would like that very much, thank you – Je veux bien, merci.
I accept (with pleasure) – J'accepte (avec plaisir).
That's very kind of you – C'est très gentil.
Yes, I would like to – Oui, je voudrais.
Okay, right, agreed – D'accord.
I'm sorry but I can't – Je regrette, mais je ne peux pas.
Make yourself at home – Faites comme chez vous.

Other Useful Phrases

Let's go – Allons, **What a surprise!** – Quelle surprise!
Good idea! – Bonne idée!, **That's it!** – Ça y est!
That's right! – C'est ça!, **Great!** – Formidable!
Oh my! – Oh là là, **Congratulations** – Félicitations!
Can I help you? – Je peux vous aider?

BISON FUTÉ

CARTE - CONSEIL ET ITINÉRAIRES BIS

Europe 2

1995 - 1996

BIS

PARTENAIRES DE BISON FUTÉ POUR 1995

COBRA - FRANCE **TELECOM** - HOTELS IBIS - McDONALD'S
NESTLÉ - NORAUTO - TELLIT DIRECT - TOTAL - VITTEL

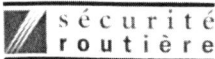

sécurité routière

Finding Your Way Around

♦ *Driving in France*

Full information on motoring in France is available from the French Government Tourist Office or the motoring organisations. The tourist office in London produces information about holiday traffic blackspots. It is produced under the cartoon heading of **Bison Futé** and is extremely useful if you have to travel in August.

Before you Leave Home

You are not allowed to drive in France on a provisional licence and the minimum age for driving is eighteen.

Make sure that your car is in the peak of condition. Faults are likely to show up because of long distances and heavy loads. Spare parts may be difficult to obtain, especially if there is a language problem. Most common faults tend to be broken brake pipes, exhaust pipes dropping off, burst hoses, bad starting and frayed or slack fanbelts. If you can take spare parts with you, you may save yourself time and worry. The motoring organisations hire out spares kits for a fee.

If you have never driven in France before and the prospect worries you, there is really very little cause for concern. Driving on the right becomes second nature after a few hours, especially since most road markings are similar to ours. There tends to be much more 'open road' in France, a lot of small villages and few large towns. Driving in towns is not too difficult as long as you avoid the rush hours, which, incidentally, seem to be slightly earlier in the morning and later in the evening than ours.

As you might expect there are situations where you do need to take extra care.

Overtaking

Special care is needed because you overtake on the left. Patience is essential, expecially when you are behind a slow farm vehicle or a caravan. Rash overtaking can be disastrous. Your front seat passenger can be of great assistance to you because in a right hand drive car the driver is often unable to see round the vehicle in front. Remember to use your left indicator when you are overtaking.

Roundabouts

For many years negotiating a roundabout in France was a very hazardous manoeuvre but at last the rule has been changed. When you approach a roundabout you will normally see the sign *Vous n'avez pas la priorité*, which says that you do not have the right of way. You have to give way to traffic which is already on the roundabout. You then join the roundabout when it is safe to do so, remembering of course that you go round to the right!

Left Turns

These are equivalent to our right turns where you take up a position on the centre line, wait for oncoming traffic to pass and then turn. Because it is natural for us to turn left almost without thinking, a momentary lack of thought on a French road can result in a head-on collision. Believe me, it is very easily done.

Priority to the Right (Priorité à droite)

This rule used to cause more trouble to English drivers than any other. Unless there is a sign saying *Passage Protégé* and halt signs on the minor roads you are passing, you must assume that side roads (mainly in built up areas) have priority and you should give way. If there is no sign at all, be prepared to give way if any vehicle comes in from the right. To English drivers this is a very silly rule and the situation has been greatly improved in recent years by halt signs on minor roads, but it pays to be cautious. If in doubt, give way. French motorists are generally fairly tolerant of our hesitancy.

Lines on Road

Do not cross single or double continuous lines. You may cross a continuous line if it has a broken line on your side. Penalties can be heavy.

Speed Limits

At the time of writing the speed limit in urban areas is 50 kmh (31 mph). On single carriageway roads the limit is 90 kmh (56 mph). If you are driving in wet weather the limit is reduced to 80 kmh (50 mph). On a dual carriageway the limit is 110 kmh (68 mph), but 100 kmh (62 mph) on a wet road. The motorway limit is 130 kmh (80mph) and 110 kmh (68 mph) in wet conditions. A minimum speed limit exists in the overtaking lane of a motorway of 80 kmh (50 mph) in daylight and good weather conditions. Local variations are indicated on speed limit road signs. The **RAPPEL** sign indicates a continuing restriction. It is advisable to check on current speed limits before you set off.

Types of Road

A – AUTOROUTE (Motorway). On most French motorways you have to pay a toll. The toll booths are called '*Péages*'. On short stretches of motorway you pay at the first *péage* but on longer stretches you take a card from a machine and pay when you leave the motorway. The further you travel, the more you pay. When you are budgeting your holiday bear in mind that motorway tolls are fairly heavy. It is possible to obtain a toll tariff from the French Government Tourist Office before you set off.

In our experience French motorways are less busy and easier

to negotiate than in the United Kingdom. Many heavy lorries do not use motorways because of the toll. However, if you can, avoid travelling on the motorways at peak holiday weekends such as the first weekend in August. The traffic queues are legendary! Motorways in the Paris region are always busy, but if you avoid rush hours you should keep moving. Motorways are well provided with picnic areas (*aires de repos*) which always have toilets, and service areas where you can buy petrol and food. For assistance on a motorway use the telephone boxes which are sited at two kilometre intervals and which are connected to local police stations.

N – ROUTE NATIONALE (Main Road). It is obviously cheaper to travel on main roads. If you are not in a hurry you will find them pleasant, straight and more interesting than motorways.

D – ROUTE DEPARTEMENTALE. These are roughly equivalent to our 'B' roads. Using them helps you to discover the real France. If you have time it is well worth the trouble.

V – CHEMIN VICINAL (Local by-road).

Please note that you are not allowed to stop on open roads unless the vehicle is driven off the road.

Seat Belts

The wearing of seat belts is compulsory in France. Children under ten are not allowed to travel in the front passenger seat.

Yellow Headlights

Headlights on French cars display a yellow beam. These are not compulsory for tourists but French drivers make life very unpleasant for British drivers who blind them with 'white lights' by sounding their horns loudly as they pass and flashing their headlights. Your car accessory shop will advise you on the best way to make your headlights yellow. The simplest way is to buy a yellow solution to paint on the glass which can be easily removed with white spirit.

Headlights on British cars usually have the beam diverted

slightly to the left. When you drive on the right, because you are on the wrong camber, your headlights shine upwards to the left and into the eyes of oncoming drivers. You should therefore try to divert your beam to the right. Beam diversion kits are now on sale at motor accessory shops. Incidentally, when a French driver flashes his headlights at you it usually means he has right of way and is coming through.

Warning Triangle

It is compulsory to carry a warning triangle, which in the event of an accident or a breakdown should be placed at the side of the carriageway about fifty metres behind the car. Triangles can be bought reasonably cheaply at car accessory shops and fit snugly into a small corner of your car boot. Make sure that it is accessible. Having to empty your boot to find it may not be very convenient when you need it urgently. Since warning triangles are quite small and may not be clearly visible in bad weather, it would be prudent to display hazard warning lights as well.

Petrol

Apart from lead-free petrol (called *sans plomb*), there are two main grades of petrol. *Essence* (often called *ordinaire*) is equivalent to 2-star and *Super* is equivalent to 3- and 4-star. If you want diesel you look for *Gas-oil*. Petrol station attendants are usually reasonably friendly and helpful. Some people tip petrol pump attendants. We never have and we have not yet encountered any hostility. Petrol is sold in litres. You can buy it by asking for the tank to be filled, or you can wave bank notes indicating that you want petrol to that value. Many French people do it this way. Do not panic if you find yourself low on petrol on a public holiday. There is always one station open, at least in the morning. Do not ask for *pétrole*. You will get paraffin. Lead-free petrol is now widely available. Some petrol pumps are operated by credit card but do not always accept international credit cards. There should be a sign on the pump.

Spare Lights Bulbs

It is compulsory for you to carry a set of replacement bulbs. It is illegal to drive with faulty lights.

Pedestrian Crossings

These have no belisha beacons. French drivers do not always give way to pedestrians. French people seem very reluctant to cross until traffic has passed. They often show surprise if you stop for them but are grateful for your courtesy. It is wise to approach pedestrian crossings with caution. They can occasionally be obscured by parked cars.

Traffic Lights

The sequence of lights is slightly different from ours. From red the light changes immediately to green, missing out red and amber. There is sometimes a traffic light on a gantry overhead as well as the one to your right, and frequently you will find an extra small set of lights at eye level on the traffic light post. Some lights permanently flash amber. Proceed with caution. Do not make yourself unpopular by stopping in a right filter lane when you are going straight on and the main light is on red.

Parking

As in Britain it can sometimes be difficult to find parking spaces in large towns and cities, especially on Saturdays and market days. The French suffer from parking restrictions and no-parking zones just as we do. Generally speaking, however, it is not normally too difficult to park. Look for the 'P' sign (white on navy blue background). Some holiday resorts even have spaces for tourist vehicles. Look for the sign **Véhicules de Tourisme Seulement**. It is often possible to park more easily in a town centre between twelve o'clock midday and two o'clock when many local people have gone home for lunch. Very busy areas sometimes display the sign **Zone Bleue – Disque Obligatoire**. You are not allowed to park in this area unless you have bought a parking disc from a *zone bleue* office, the town hall, the tourist office or a tobacconists.

YOU MAY PARK WHERE YOU SEE THE FOLLOWING SIGNS

Parking voitures – **Parking for cars.**
Parking libre/gratuit – **Free parking.**
Stationnement permanent – **Permanent parking.**
Parking Souterrain – **Underground car park.**
Parc de stationnement pour tous véhicules – **Car park for all vehicles.**
Côté de stationnement – **You may park on this side of the road.**
Stationnement Bilateral Autorisé – **Parking authorised on both sides.**
Parking des deux côtés – **Parking on both sides.**
Stationnement alterné semi-mensuel – **Parking on alternate sides on a fortnightly basis (look for dates).**
Parking payant horodateur – **Pay and display car park.**
Fin d'interdiction de stationnement – **End of parking restrictions.**

YOU MAY NOT PARK WHERE YOU SEE THE FOLLOWING SIGNS:

Ne pas stationner . . .
Parking interdit . . .
Prière de ne pas stationner . . .
Stationnement interdit . . .
Défense de stationner . . .
Interdiction de stationnement . . . (**All mean 'no parking'**).
Stationnement réservé aux poids lourds – **Parking reserved for heavy lorries.**
Accès interdit aux voitures particulières – **No access for private vehicles.**
Rue or voie piétonne – **Pedestrian street or precinct.**

Zone d'enlèvement des véhicules – **Towing away zone**.
Stationnement interdit le mardi de 7h à 14h – **No parking on Tuesdays from 7 a.m. to 2 p.m. (usually because of market day)**.
Interdit sur trottoir – **No parking on the pavement**.

Police

Traffic police patrol widely and are often in evidence making spot checks on vehicles. On-the-spot fines are imposed on drivers who cross white lines, have overloaded vehicles and break speed limits. They are very severe with drivers who are under the influence of alcohol. There are frequent random breath tests. I was once stopped and warned for failing to display headlights in a short, well-lit tunnel! The French Tourist Office will advise you about the amount of fines you have to pay for traffic violations.

Pedestrians

Remember that while you are on holiday in France you will be a pedestrian as well as a driver. Exercise extreme caution on pedestrian crossings and remember to look LEFT when crossing the road. At a controlled pedestrian crossing you will come across the signs *Attendez* (wait) and *Traversez* (cross).

Caravans

There are no formalities for the temporary importation of touring caravans for a stay in France of up to six months. Any vehicle towing a caravan must, by law, be fitted with wing mirrors. The maximum gross weight of the caravan should not exceed the kerbside weight of the towing vehicle without passengers. When towing a caravan on a motorway the driver must, by law, make sure that he is driving at least fifty yards behind the vehicle in front. There are sometimes extra speed restrictions for caravans on steep downward slopes. They are well marked and should be observed.

Motor Cycles and Mopeds

You are not allowed to ride a moped on motorways. You must have insurance and a crash helmet must be worn. The minimum age is 14 and no licence is needed.

For motorcycles between 81cc and 400cc the minimum age is 18. You need a full licence and the speed limit is as for cars.

For large motorcycles over 400cc a heavy motorcycle licence is required. The minimum age is 18 and the speed limit is as for cars.

All motorcycles must have registration plates, GB plates and at least third party insurance. Crash helmets must be worn by drivers and passengers and dipped headlights must be used at all times except when stationary.

In the Event of an Accident

If you have a minor accident, keep calm. Language difficulties can cause problems which are more easily resolved in a calm atmosphere. French motorists tend to become excitable and argumentative. Do not admit liability. At the scene of an accident you should fill in a *Constat Amiable*, a European accident statement. An English version of this should be included with your insurance green card. Your insurance company will advise you on what particulars to include and it would be wise to be familiar with the procedure before you go. Keep the form in your car.

Road Signs

You will find the following road signs useful:

Carrefour – **Crossroads**	Centre-ville – **Town Centre**
Chaussée Déformée – **Uneven surface**	Déviation – **Diversion**
Feux rouges – **Traffic lights**	Gas-oil – **Diesel**

Gravillons – **Loose chippings**

Péage – **Motorway pay toll**

Priorité à droite – **Give way to right**

Rappel! – **Caution restriction applies**

Roulez lentement – **Drive slowly**

Sens interdit – **No entry**

Serrez à droite – **Keep to the right**

Station service – **Petrol station**

Virage – **Bend**

Passage Protégé – **Your priority is protected by halt signs on side roads**

Poids Lourds – **Heavy lorries**

Ralentir (Ralentissez) – **Slow down**

Route barrée – **Road blocked**

Sens unique – **One way street**

Sortie de camions – **Exit for lorries**

Toutes directions – **All thro' traffic**

Useful Motoring Vocabulary

Les pneus – **Tyres**, La batterie – **Battery**
L'essence – **Petrol**, Le volant – **Steering wheel**
L'huile – **Oil**, Les phares – **Headlights**
L'eau – **Water**, Les vitesses – **Gears**
Le moteur – **Engine**, Les freins – **Brakes**
Le pare-brise – **Windscreen**, L'embrayage – **Clutch**
Les bougies – **Plugs**, L'essuie-glace – **Windscreen wipers**
Le delco – **Distributor**, La courroie de ventilateur – **Fan belt**

What to say at a Petrol Station

Is there a petrol station near here? – Il y a une station service près d'ici?
Is it self-service? – C'est libre service?

Fill it up with four star/two star/unleaded – Faites le plein de super/d'ordinaire/de sans plomb.

Forty litres of four star – Quarante litres de super.

A hundred francs worth of four star – Cent francs de super.

Will you check the water/oil/tyre pressures/battery? – Voulez-vous vérifier l'eau/l'huile/la pression des pneus/la batterie?

Will you wipe the windscreen? – Voulez-vous essuyer le pare-brise?

Have you a map of the region? – Avez-vous une carte de la région?

Is this the right road for . . .? – C'est bien la route de . . .?

Which direction is it for . . .? – C'est quelle direction pour . . .?

What to say if you have a problem with the car

Can you help me please? – Pouvez-vous m'aider, s'il vous plaît?

Can you send a mechanic please? – Pouvez-vous envoyer un mécanicien, s'il vous plaît?

I am on the main road 16 – Je suis sur la Route Nationale 16.

Twenty kilometres from Rouen – Vingt kilomètres de Rouen.

It is a blue Ford – C'est une Ford bleue.

The registration number is – Le numéro d'immatriculation est.

I am broken down – Je suis en panne.

I have run out of petrol – Je suis en panne d'essence.

Do you do repairs? – Vous faites des réparations?

Will you look at my car? – Voulez-vous regarder ma voiture?

My car won't start – Ma voiture ne démarre pas.

I have a puncture – J'ai un pneu crevé.

Can you repair it? – Pouvez-vous le réparer?

I have lost the key – J'ai perdu la clé.

The engine is not working properly – Le moteur ne marche pas bien.

The brakes are not working – Les freins ne marchent pas.

The indicators are not working – Les clignotants ne marchent pas.

The clutch is not working – L'embrayage ne fonctionne pas.

The windscreen wiper is not working – L'essuie-glace ne fonctionne pas.

Horaire

du / 29 Sept
au / 30 Mai

SNCF 320

Paris – Le Havre

- Paris
- Mantes-la-Jolie
- Vernon
- Gaillon-Aubevoye
- Val-de-Reuil
- Oissel
- Rouen
- Yvetot
- Bréauté-Beuzeville
- Le Havre

- Le Havre
- Bréauté-Beuzeville
- Yvetot
- Rouen
- Oissel
- Val-de-Reuil
- Gaillon-Aubevoye
- Vernon
- Mantes-la-Jolie
- Paris

MANTES-LA-JOLIE - PARIS-ST-LAZARE PAR POISSY

	▲	▲	A	A	C	A	A	A	A	C	A
MANTES-LA-JOLIE	4.18	4.48	5.14	5.37	5.58	6.00	6.18	6.20	6.42	6.58	6.58
Mantes Station	4.21	4.51	5.17	5.39	6.01	6.02		6.22	6.43	7.01	
Epône Mézières	4.27	4.57	5.23	5.46	6.07	6.09		6.29	6.49	7.07	
Aubergenville	4.31	5.01	5.27	5.50	6.10	6.13		6.33	6.53	7.10	
Les Mureaux	4.36	5.06	5.32	5.55	6.15	6.19		6.39	6.59	7.15	
Poissy	4.53	5.23	5.49	6.12	6.32					7.32	
PARIS-ST-LAZARE	5.20	5.50	6.12	6.32	6.52	6.51	6.53	7.11	7.31	7.52	7.33

▲ tous les jours · **A** tous les jours sauf sam., dim. et fêtes · **C** sam., dim. et fêtes · **S** samedi ·
dim. et fêtes · **A1** tous les jours sauf sam., dim. et fêtes et sauf les 31.10 et 26.5 ·

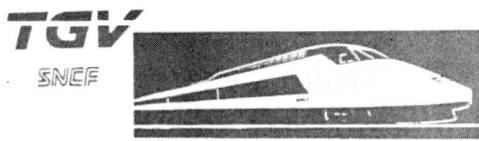

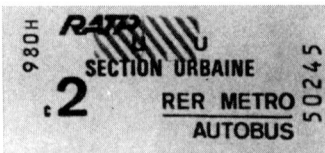

The fan belt needs replacing – Il faut remplacer la courroie de ventilateur.

I am using too much petrol/oil – Je dépense trop d'essence/d'huile.

Can you repair the car right away? – Pouvez-vous réparer la voiture tout de suite?

When will the car be ready? – Quand est-ce que la voiture sera prête?

How much will it cost? – Combien est-ce que cela coûtera?

How much do I owe you? – Je vous dois combien?

♦ *Making Use of Public Transport*

Travelling by Train

The French railway system is called the *Société Nationale des Chemins de Fer Français (S.N.C.F.)*. After a massive modernisation programme which was made necessary by Allied bombing during the Second World War when a large part of the railway network was destroyed, France today has one of the most modern and efficient railway systems in the world. It runs on 35,000 kilometres of mostly electrified tracks. Its trains are fast, comfortable and punctual!

The pride of the S.N.C.F. is the *Train à Grande Vitesse (T.G.V.)*, a long distance train, which provides a service between Paris and the large cities. It has double-glazed, air-conditioned, pleasantly decorated carriages and runs at a maximum speed of three hundred kilometres per hour. All seats have to be reserved in advance and passengers have their reservation fee refunded if it arrives late, which it rarely does.

The two standard main line units are called *Corails*, which are pulled by electric locomotives and *Turbotrains*, powered by gas turbine engines. There are three main types of train on French Railways. *Un Rapide* is a fast express train which only stops at important stations and for which there is usually a supplement. *Un Express* is a fast train which stops at main stations and *Un*

Omnibus is a red and yellow branch line diesel train used for short journeys and stopping at all stations.

Hardly anyone seems to pay full price for tickets. There are all kinds of concessions: there is a reduction for journeys above 1,500 kilometres, there are large reductions for families with three children or more and for elderly and disabled people. Children under four travel free and groups can negotiate a special rate. For further information write to French Railways, 179 Piccadilly, London.

An S.N.C.F. timetable is called a *Chaix* after the man who first published it. You can buy one at the station. You can also buy a pocket timetable called a *Fiche Horaire*. A railway ticket shows the destination, the cost of the ticket, the class and whether it is a single or a return. A reserved seat has a different, larger ticket with information about the journey displayed on the top half and details of the reservation on the lower half. You must remember to *compost* your ticket before you go on to the platform. A *Composteur* is an orange coloured machine which punches and dates your ticket. Once dated the ticket is only valid on that day. It is important to keep the ticket when you get on to the train in case the *Contrôleur* wants to check it.

If you need to find your way around a railway station you will find the following signs useful:

Consigne – **Left luggage office**, Salle d'attente – **Waiting room**
Guichet des billets – **Ticket office**, Composteur – **Ticket machine**
Passage souterrain – **Subway**, Horaire – **Timetable**
Buffet/Buvette – **Restaurant/snacks**, Quais – **Platforms**
Indicateur or Panneau de départ – **Departure board**, Bureau de renseignements – **Information office**
Bureau du chef de gare – **Stationmaster's office**, Bureau des objets trouvés – **Lost property office**

What to Say when Catching a Train

How do I get to the station please? – Pour aller à la gare, s'il vous plaît?

I would like a single ticket – Je voudrais un billet simple.

A return ticket to Rouen please – Un aller et retour pour Rouen, s'il vous plaît.

A first/second class ticket – Un billet de première/seconde classe.

How much is a second class ticket? – C'est combien un billet de deuxième classe?

What platform is it for Paris? – Pour Paris, c'est quel quai?

What platform does the Paris train leave from? – Le train pour Paris part de quel quai?

I'd like to reserve a seat – Je voudrais réserver une place.

I'd like a seat near the window – Je voudrais une place près de la fenêtre.

I'd prefer a no-smoking compartment – Je préfère un compartiment non-fumeur.

I'd like to leave this morning/this afternoon/this evening/tomorrow – Je voudrais partir ce matin/cet après-midi/ce soir/demain.

What time does the train leave? – Le train part à quelle heure?

Is there a train later/earlier? – Il y a un train plus tard/plus tôt?

I've missed the train to . . . – J'ai manqué le train pour . . .

Is there another train today? – Il y a un autre train aujourd'hui?

Is it a through train? – C'est direct?

What time does the train arrive at . . .? – A quelle heure est-ce que le train arrive à . . .?

Do I have to change trains? – Il faut changer?

Where do I change? – Où est-ce que je change?

Is this the right train for Angers? – C'est bien le train pour Angers?

Is there a restaurant car? – Il y a un wagon-restaurant?

Is this seat vacant? – Cette place est libre?

Is the train on time/late? – Le train est à l'heure/en retard?

Travelling on the Paris Métro

When you are in Paris, trying to do as much sight-seeing as possible, the quickest way of getting about is on the Paris underground, the *Métropolitain* or *Métro* for short. There are over three hundred and fifty stations and the lines usually follow the direction of the main avenues of Paris. The stations are well signposted and are closer together than those on the London Underground.

At each Métro station you will find large plans of the system. You can also obtain small plans free of charge from the ticket office or from a tourist information office. The lines are colour-coded and each one has a number and two names, which are the last stations at each end of the line. In the stations and on the platforms themselves you will see signs displaying the number and name of each line. To get to any station on a certain line you follow the direction of the station at the end of the line.

If you have to change trains because your destination is on a different line from the one on which you started, you get off at the station where the two lines intersect. You then look for the yellow sign *Correspondance* (connections), which you follow to the next platform where you again look for the last station on the new line in the direction you want to go.

Certain seats at the end of each compartment are reserved for various categories of disabled people and for pregnant women. As a tourist you would be well advised to avoid using the Métro during the rush hours between seven and nine o'clock in the morning and five and seven in the evening, when it is extremely busy transporting commuters to and from work.

An important safety feature in Métro stations is the *Portillon Automatique*, a gate at the end of the platform which closes automatically as a train comes into the station and prevents people from rushing onto a train at the last minute.

There is one basic fare in the Métro no matter what distance you cover, and one ticket only is now sufficient to cover any journey within Paris. A ticket is yellow and can be used on a bus as well as on the Métro. If you intend to make several trips over a period of days it would be advantageous to buy a *Carnet* of ten tickets. On the reverse side of each ticket there is a magnetic strip. As you pass through the automatic ticket barrier you put your ticket in the slot and it is electronically cancelled and returned to you. You cannot use the same ticket twice and the barrier will remain closed if you try to. Because it is possible to cheat the barrier machines there are frequent spot checks, so it is wise to hang onto your ticket until you leave the Métro.

What to Say When Travelling on the Métro

Is there a métro station near here? – Il y a une station de métro près d'ici?
Have you got a métro plan? – Vous avez un plan de métro?
Is it free of charge? – C'est gratuit?
Which station is it for Notre Dame? – C'est quelle station pour Notre Dame?
A ticket please – Un billet, s'il vous plaît.
A second class ticket – Un billet de deuxième classe.
A book of tickets – Un carnet de billets.
Is this the right line for . . .? – C'est bien la ligne pour . . .?
Which direction should I take? – Je dois prendre quelle direction?
How do I get to Louvre, please? – Pour aller à Louvre, s'il vous plaît?
What should I do? – Qu'est-ce qu'il faut faire?
Do I need to change? – Il faut changer?
Do I get off here for the Arc de Triomphe? – On descend ici pour L'Arc de Triomphe?
Excuse me, I'm getting off here – Excusez-moi, je descends ici.
What time is the last métro train? – A quelle heure est le dernier métro?

Travelling by Bus

In Paris the bus service is run by the *Régie Autonome des Transports Parisiens (R.A.T.P.)*, which also includes the Métro. Tickets are interchangeable. Bus timetables and plans (*un Plan des Autobus*) can be bought at newspaper shops and certain other shops which display the R.A.T.P. sign. Buses usually display a plan of the bus route and you can also check your route from the information on the back of a bus stop. On the front of a bus stop is displayed the number and name of the stop. If you are intending to travel frequently on buses it is advisable to buy *Carnets* of tickets. You can buy tickets from the bus driver as you get on the bus, but it is cheaper to buy them in advance. When you have paid the driver or got on the bus with tickets purchased elsewhere you have your ticket punched in the ticket machine which will be situated near the driver. Certain seats are reserved for handicapped people and *mutilés de guerre* (people disabled during the War). There is usually lots of standing room on buses, but in the rush hours it may be better to walk. French buses are mostly single deckers, with the exception of a few buses in Paris. You get on at the front door and get off in the middle. There are two types of bus stop, an *arrêt facultatif* where the bus only stops if you signal, and an *arrêt obligatoire* where the bus is obliged to stop.

In towns other than Paris, buses usually run from the *Gare D'Autobus* (bus station) and cross-country buses and excursion coaches from the *Gare Routière*. Most towns have one or the other. Only large towns have both. Very small towns and villages may not have either. Buses tend to leave from the main square or the market place.

What to Say when Catching a Bus or a Coach

Is the bus station near here? – La gare d'autobus est près d'ici?
How do I get to the bus station? – Pour aller à la gare routière?
Which bus goes to . . .? – Quel est l'autobus pour . . .?
Which line is it to go to . . .? – C'est quelle ligne pour aller à . . .?
Is this the right bus for the station? – C'est bien l'autobus pour la gare?
I'd like to go to . . . – Je voudrais aller à . . .
How frequent are the buses? – Il y a un autobus tous les combien?
Is there a bus stop nearby? – Il y a un arrêt d'autobus près d'ici?
To go to the station, where do I get off? – Pour aller à la gare, où est-ce que je descends?

VISITE DE LA VILLE

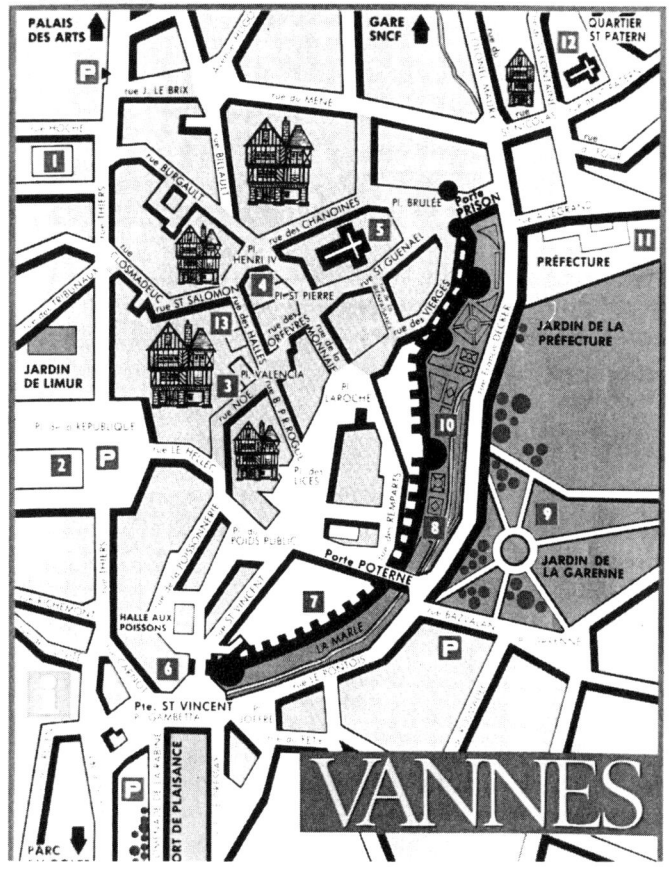

Does the bus stop at the station? – Est-ce que l'autobus s'arrête à la gare?

Which stop is it for the station? – C'est quel arrêt pour la gare?

Is it the next stop? – C'est le prochain arrêt?

Will you tell me when I arrive at my stop? – Voulez-vous me dire quand j'arrive à mon arrêt?

Is there a coach for Dieppe today? – Il y a un car pour Dieppe aujourd'hui?

It's for tomorrow – C'est pour demain.

Have you any bus tickets? – Avez-vous des billets d'autobus?

A single ticket to Dieppe – Un aller simple pour Dieppe.

A return ticket to Dieppe – Un aller et retour pour Dieppe.

Is this the right coach for Dieppe? – C'est bien le car pour Dieppe?

What time does the first/next/last coach leave? – A quelle heure part le premier/prochain/dernier car?

What time does it arrive? – Il arrive à quelle heure?

♦ *Finding your Way Around on Foot*

When you arrive in a French town, in order to find your way around you should call in at the local tourist office, the *Syndicat d'Initiative* or the *Office de Tourisme*. They produce excellent leaflets containing information about accommodation, entertainments, restaurants, transport, excursions, places of interest, sports facilities, doctors, chemists and other emergency services. They also invariably give you a street plan of the town. The literature is always given free of charge. Usually the staff are very pleasant and helpful. It is likely that someone will speak English but they are always pleased when you try out your French. You can revert back to English if you get into difficulties, but the tourist office is the one place where your efforts to speak French will be greeted sympathetically.

The important places in a town are usually indicated by signs which have navy blue lettering on a white background. Here are some of the main ones:

Auberge de Jeunesse – **Youth Hostel**

Bibliothèque – **Library**

Camping – **Campsite**

Cathédrale – **Cathedral**

Centre Commercial – **Shopping centre**

Centre ville – **Town centre**

Château – **Castle**

Clinique – **Hospital**

Collège – **Secondary school**

Commissariat – **Police station**

École – **School**

Église – **Church**

Gare (S.N.C.F.) – **Railway station**

Gare d'autobus – **Bus station**

Gare Routière – **Bus station**

Gendarmerie – **Police station**

Hôpital – **Hospital**

Hôtel de ville – **Town hall**

Jardin public – **Park**

Lycée – **Sixth Form College**

Mairie – **Town hall (small)**

Maison de la culture – **Cultural centre**

Maison des jeunes – **Youth club**

Marché – **Market**

Musée – **Museum**

Office de tourisme – **Tourist office**

Palais de justice – **Law courts**

Parc – **Park**

Parking – **Car park**

Piscine – **Swimming pool**

Place du marché – **Market place**

Pompiers – **Fire brigade**

Pont – **Bridge**

Poste – **Post office**

Poste de police – **Police station**

Préfecture – **Prefect's headquarters**

Stade – **Stadium**

Station de métro – **Métro station**

Syndicat d'initiative – **Information office**

Terrain de sport – **Sports ground**

Toilettes (W.C.) – **Toilets**

Vieux Quartier – **Old district**

Zone Piétonne – **Pedestrian precinct**

What to Say at the Tourist Office and in the Street

Where is the tourist office? – Où est le syndicat d'initiative?

Can you help me? – Pouvez-vous m'aider?

Have you any tourist leaflets? – Avez-vous des dépliants touristiques?

Have you got a town plan? – Avez-vous un plan de la ville?

I need a list of hotels/campsites – J'ai besoin d'une liste d'hôtels/de campings.

I am looking for a reasonably priced hotel – Je cherche un hôtel modeste.

Speak more slowly, please – Parlez plus lentement, s'il vous plaît.

I do not understand – Je ne comprends pas.

Will you repeat? – Voulez-vous répéter?

I am lost – Je suis perdu.

I am looking for – Je cherche.

Excuse me, Sir, how do I get to the post office? – Pardon, Monsieur, pour aller à la poste?

Is the post office far? – La poste, c'est loin?

Is the information office nearby? – Le syndicat d'initiative, c'est près?

Is there a . . . near here? – Il y a un(e) . . . près d'ici?

Where is the nearest . . .? – Où est le/la . . . le/la plus proche?

Where is there a car park? – Où est-ce qu'il y a un parking?

How far is it? – C'est à quelle distance?

Have you a bus timetable? – Vous avez un horaire des bus?

Where can I hire . . .? – Où est-ce que je peux louer . . .?

Can we get there on foot? – Est-ce qu'on peut y aller à pied?

Money Matters

Before you set off you need to decide how much French currency to take, how much English money and whether to take travellers' cheques or Eurocheques. We have always relied on a combination of French francs, English pounds and travellers' cheques. We take French currency (perhaps £100 worth) to tide us over the first few days without having to look for a bank. We have English money, not particularly to spend, but to have in reserve just in case.

Travellers' Cheques

The bulk of our spending money is in travellers' cheques because their value can be reclaimed if they are lost or stolen. We usually take about £200 more than we have budgeted for, taking into consideration campsite fees, food, petrol, motorway tolls, wine and spirits to bring home and spending money. It is simpler doing that than having to contact the British Consul in order to have extra money sent out from Britain in an emergency. It is also nice to be able to bring some money back from a holiday.

The next consideration is whether to have travellers' cheques in Sterling or in French francs. There are arguments in favour of either. If you know you will spend all your travellers' cheques it is prudent to buy them in francs, because you will receive the face value of them (often without paying any commission at all). If, however, you bring some back you will lose quite heavily on the exchange rate when you cash them. Buying Sterling cheques works in the opposite way. You lose when you cash them in France, but you receive the face value if you cash them in this country. Your own bank will of course advise you about travellers' cheques but you can obtain them over the counter quite easily from travel agencies. Your bank may require a week's notice.

Eurocheques

Many people now use Eurocheques and find them very convenient for paying campsite fees, hotel, restaurant and supermarket bills, also for petrol. They reduce the need to find a bank or to carry large amounts of cash. However, check very carefully with your bank before taking Eurocheques as apparently some French banks have suffered fraud losses and are now refusing to accept them.

Banks

Some of the best known banks are the *Crédit Lyonnais*, the *Crédit Agricole*, the *Société Générale* and the *Banque Nationale de Paris*, but there are others and banks tend to be fairly close together in the main shopping streets of towns. Whichever bank you choose you need to look out for the sign *Change* in the window and probably a list of currencies and exchange rates.

Most banks have regular opening hours, but you would be wise to check closing days and bank holidays. There is nothing worse than being short of cash when the banks are closed, especially if you are low on petrol. Establishments will not accept travellers' cheques instead of cash.

Bureaux de Change

Two other places where you can change money are the *Bureau de Change* and some large hypermarkets. *Bureaux de Change* are usually situated centrally in popular holiday resorts. We avoid them. We feel that they do not give a good rate of exchange, but worse, there is usually a high commission charged for the transaction. If you plan ahead you will not need to use them. Equally, it can be a gamble changing money in a hypermarket. Some give a good exchange rate on the premise that you are going to give them the money back anyway by shopping there. Others, whilst having an attractive exchange rate, may charge a large commission.

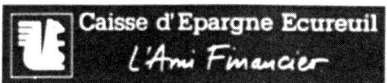

avec elle j'avance
114 et 116, avenue de Royat - Tél. 73 35 91 05
Bureaux ouverts du mardi au samedi

Crédit♻Mutuel

une banque à qui parler

35, avenue de Royat - Tél. **73 30 91 60**

Credit Cards

French credit cards have a chip which contains identification information. Cards from Britain contain the same information on a magnetic strip but French card reading machines do not always pick it up. The French Tourist Office advises British Tourists to write the following on a piece of paper and to produce it with their passport when presenting a credit card:

'Les cartes Anglaises ne sont pas des cartes à puce, mais à bande magnétique. Ma carte est valable et je vous serais reconnaissant d'en demander la confirmation auprès de votre banque ou de votre centre de traitement.'

This explains that your card is valid.

What the Bank Employee Might Say to You

Combien voulez-vous changer? – **How much do you want to change?**
C'est pour les livres sterling ou les chèques de voyage? – **Is it for English pounds or travellers' cheques?**
Vous avez votre passeport? – **Have you got your passport?**
Vous avez une pièce d'identité? – **Have you any identification?**
Signez le formulaire, s'il vous plaît – **Sign the form please.**
Présentez ce papier à la caisse – **Take this paper to the cash desk.**
Voulez-vous passer à la caisse? – **Will you go to the cash desk?**
Vous avez une carte bancaire? – **Have you got a bank card?**

What to Say When Changing Money

Je cherche une banque – **I am looking for a bank.**
Il y a une banque près d'ici? – **Is there a bank near here?**
La banque est ouverte? – **Is the bank open?**
La banque ferme à quelle heure? – **What times does the bank close?**
Je peux changer (cent) livres sterling en francs? – **Can I change (a hundred) pounds into francs?**

Je voudrais changer des chèques de voyage en francs – **I would like to change some travellers' cheques into francs.**

Je peux encaisser un chèque de voyage? – **Can I cash a travellers' cheque?**

Quel est le taux de change aujourd'hui? – **What is the exchange rate today?**

La livre est à combien aujourd'hui? – **How much is the pound worth today?**

Voici mon passeport – **Here is my passport.**

Voudriez-vous me donner des billets de cent (de cinquante) francs? – **Please would you give me hundred (fifty) franc notes?**

Je voudrais quelques pièces de dix francs – **I would like a few ten franc coins.**

Eating Out

♦ Buying a Drink or a Snack in a Café

A French café is roughly equivalent to a British pub but there are many differences. French licensing hours, for example, are very flexible and very convenient for tourists who can buy a drink when they choose. Cafés only have to close in the early hours of the morning. In reality, the owner usually opens early in the morning at about seven o'clock to attract customers on their way to work and closes when the last customer leaves. Cafés tend to close earlier in small towns and villages, especially on a Sunday evening. Unlike many pubs in Britain children are welcome in cafés if accompanied by adults. Age is not important, except that spirits cannot be sold to anyone under the age of eighteen. In France, just as the café proprietor is trusted to use his discretion about opening times, so parents are trusted to take responsibility for what their children drink. Unaccompanied children may buy drinks from the age of sixteen.

There are several types of café. A *Bar* only sells drinks. A *Brasserie* sells food as well as drinks. A *Café-restaurant* serves drinks, snacks and also full meals. The type of food on sale in a café varies but often it is crusty sandwiches, hot-dogs, omelettes, *Crêpes* (pancakes), *Frites* (chips), *Croques-Monsieur* (toasted cheese sandwiches) and *Glaces* (ice creams).

When you enter a café it is usual to sit down at a table inside or outside on the *Terrasse*. The waiter will come to you and serve you at the table. However, you can buy drinks at the bar if you wish and prices are sometimes slightly cheaper. As a rule, French waiters are very efficient and polite. You can attract their attention in a busy bar by indicating with your hand or by calling '*Monsieur*'.

When your drinks are brought the waiter will normally leave the bill on the table. If you pay right away, he will tear the bill to show that it has been paid. Some waiters do not bring a bill until you are ready to leave even if you have had several rounds of drinks. Many British tourists are unsure about whether to leave a tip and how much. If the bill says *Service Compris* or *Prix Net* you do not need to leave a tip. If it says *Service Non Compris* or *Service à l'appréciation de la clientèle* it is usual to leave a tip of not less than ten and no more than fifteen per cent. If it is not clear from the bill whether the service is included or not, you can ask *Le service est compris?* If the answer is no, you will be expected to leave a tip.

In most cafés, you will see displayed a drinks list called *Boissons Pilotes* or *Tarif de Consommations* which show which drinks are on sale, the measures and the prices. You may find the following measures helpful:

Le verre – **Glass**	La tasse – **Cup**
Le litre – **Litre**	Le demi (litre) – **Half (a litre)**
Le quart – **Quarter of a litre**	La bouteille – **Bottle**

Some drinks may be advertised in centilitres (c.l.). There are about seventy to seventy five centilitres in a normal size bottle of wine.

The drinks sold in French cafés are many and varied – enough to give you an excuse for frequent visits! Having a drink in a French café is one of the most enjoyable French experiences, whether it be a mid-morning cup of coffee, an apéritif before lunch, a cool drink on a hot afternoon or a social evening occasion. *A votre santé!*

Choose your Drinks from this List

Boissons Pilotes

Bière (à la pression) – **Draught beer**, Bière (en bouteille) – **Bottled beer**

Bière brune – **Brown Ale**, Cidre – **Cider**
Vin rouge – **Red wine**, Vin rosé – **Rosé wine**
Vin blanc (sec, demi-sec, doux) – **White wine (dry, medium dry, sweet)**, Vin mousseux (or pétillant) – **Sparkling wine**
Café au lait – **Large breakfast cup of white coffee**
Café crème – **Small white coffee served at any time of day**
Café express – **Very strong small black coffee**
Café filtre – **Very strong ground coffee served through a filter**
Café – **Small black coffee**
Thé – **Tea (only served with milk if you ask for it)**
Tisane – **An infused drink made like tea with leaves and flowers**
Flavours – Tilleul (**lime**), Camomille, Menthe (**mint**)
Lait – **Milk**
Chocolat – **Cocoa or chocolate drink**
Sirops (menthe, citron, etc.) – **Cordials (mint, lemon, etc.)**
Diabolo menthe – **Mint cordial with lemonade**
Orangina – **Very popular fizzy drink**
Limonade, Orangeade – **Lemonade, orangeade**
Jus de fruit – **Fruit juice**
Flavours – Orange, Pamplemousse (**grapefruit**), Ananas (**pineapple**), Citron (**lemon**), Cassis (**blackcurrant**)
Citron pressé – **Freshly squeezed lemon juice**
Eau minérale (gazeuse) – **Mineral water (sparkling)** – Some of the most well known are Vittel, Evian, Vichy, Perrier, Contrexéville

Apéritifs (Drinks to have before a meal as an appetizer)

Pastis, Pernod, Ricard – **Aniseed based spirits taken with water or ice.**
Vermouths – **Dubonnet, Cinzano, Martini, Noilly Prat (very dry), St. Raphael (red sweet, white dry and white ambré flavoured with bitter orange)**
Suze – **A yellow bitter tasting drink, not to everyone's taste**
Byrrh – **A bitter sweet apéritif not unlike Dubonnet**

Digestifs and Liqueurs

Cognac, Armagnac – **Brandies**
Calvados – **Very strong apple brandy from Normandy**
Chartreuse – **Green (sometimes yellow) liqueur made from herbs**
Bénédictine – **A liqueur made in Normandy**
Cointreau – **A sweet liqueur made from orange peel**
Marie Brizard – **A very sweet aniseed liqueur drunk with ice**

What to Say in a Café

Waiter, please! – Monsieur (Mademoiselle), s'il vous plaît!
I would like – Je voudrais
I want – Je veux
I'll have – Je vais prendre
Give me – Donnez-moi
Bring me – Apportez-moi
A cup of tea – Une tasse de thé
A cup of coffee – Une tasse de café
A glass of beer – Un verre de bière
A glass of white wine – Un verre de vin blanc
A glass of lemonade – Un verre de limonade
A bottle of orangina – Une bouteille d'orangina
A bottle of beer – Une bouteille de bière
A coca-cola, please – Un coca-cola, s'il vous plaît
A beer and a red wine – Une bière et un vin rouge
Have you any ice? – Avez-vous des glaçons?
I would like a spoon – Je voudrais une cuillère
I need some sugar/milk – Il me faut du sucre/du lait
What have you got in the way of sandwiches? – Qu'est-ce que vous avez comme sandwiches?
A ham sandwich – Un sandwich au jambon
A cheese sandwich – Un sandwich au fromage
A pâté sandwich – Un sandwich au pâté
A salami sandwich – Un sandwich au saucisson
A toasted cheese sandwich – Un croque-monsieur
I'd like the bill please – Je voudrais l'addition, s'il vous plaît

How much is it? – C'est combien?
Is the service included? – Le service est compris?
Where are the toilets, please? – Où sont les toilettes, s'il vous plaît?

A conversation in a café might proceed as follows:

Waiter: Bonjour. Qu'est-ce que vous prenez? (What are you having?)

Customer: Bonjour. Deux cafés au lait, s'il vous plaît.

Waiter: Oui, Monsieur, tout de suite (right away).

Customer: Qu'est-ce que vous avez comme sandwiches?

Waiter: Euh, des sandwiches au pâté, au fromage et au jambon.

Customer: Je voudrais un sandwich au jambon, s'il vous plaît.

Waiter: Oui, Monsieur.

Customer: Et apportez-moi l'addition, s'il vous plaît.

♦ *Restaurants*

French cuisine has a world wide reputation and eating in a restaurant is an experience not to be missed. Besides the top class restaurants there are many others which serve excellent food at reasonable prices. Avoid restaurants which look empty. Try to find out from the locals where they eat out. In popular areas it is a good idea to get away from the 'tourist' restaurants and search one out in a side street. A humble looking establishment may well have higher standards of cookery than a grand-looking place. It is very rare to find a restaurant which serves English food, although if that is what you want there are burger bars and fast food *brasseries*. Menus are normally displayed outside restaurants.

Restaurants are usually open between noon and about two thirty and in the evening from about seven o'clock. You may find the service slow compared with what you are used to in this country. This tends to be because eating is a leisurely activity in

France and if you are in a rush you would be advised not to have a restaurant meal.

Wine is not usually included in the price of a meal and the mark-up on wine varies as it does here. It can be cheaper to ask for the house wine rather than bottles from the menu. You can ask for ordinary water of course (*de l'eau fraîche*) but you can also buy purified water (*Vittel, Evian, Perrier*, etc.) if you prefer it. *Apéritifs* (drinks before a meal) and *Digestifs* (drinks which help you to digest a meal) can be expensive. If you have children who cannot manage a full meal ask the waiter to share it between them or order one main course and ask for an extra plate.

Other Types of Eating Place

Brasserie – **A pub which sells sandwiches and snacks**.
Casse-Croûte – **A snack bar**.
Salon de thé – **A tea room which will probably be quite expensive**.
Bistro – **Usually a small cheap restaurant but in Paris could be smart and expensive**.
Relais Routiers – **A lorry drivers' transport café which serves good food at reasonable prices and provides cheap accommodation**.
Un self – **A self-service restaurant**.
Crêperie – **A pancake stall or restaurant. Make sure you try some of the many savoury and sweet fillings**.

Types of Menu

Most restaurants have two types of menu, a fixed price menu – *Menu à prix fixe* and an *à la carte* menu. The difference is that the fixed price menu offers a choice of first course, main course and dessert and you pay one price which is displayed at the top of the menu. On an *à la carte* menu every item is priced separately and you pay for each item chosen. Fixed price menus give good value for money but *à la carte* menus give you much more choice. Try to find an excuse to have at least one *à la carte* meal during your stay. Two other types of menu you may come across are a *menu conseillé* (recommended menu) and a *menu touristique* (tourist menu). These are both fixed price menus and each one should be judged on its merits. Some restaurants have several fixed price menus at different prices. You choose the one which suits your wallet. You may decide that your children will have a cheap one and you have a more expensive one.

Different Eating Habits

When you eat out in France you will notice that the table is set differently than in England. There may be two or three wine glasses. There will be no side plate. The fork may be placed prongs downwards. There may be a knife rest to prevent the table cloth from being soiled. There will be no cups and saucers on the table. Unless you have soup you will probably be expected to use the same plate for your starter and main course. It is possible that vegetables may not be served at the same time as the meat course. Bread and water will be provided without charge. You can always ask for more bread. Bread is usually broken with the fingers and placed on the table. It is common to see French people cut up food with their knife in their right hand, put the knife down, transfer the fork to the right hand and push food onto the fork with a piece of bread. Steak and lamb tend to be undercooked, so it is no use complaining if it looks raw, unless you stress that you want it *bien cuit* (well done). It is usual for the cheese course to be served before the dessert. Desserts often consist of fruit, yoghurt or ice cream. Remember that *merci* means 'no, thank you' until you have received what is being offered.

Menu Terms

These phrases will help you to be able to read a menu:

Au choix – **A choice of**   Boissons – **Drinks**

Carte de vins – **Wine list**   Couvert (compris) – **Cover charge included**

Petit déjeuner – **Breakfast**

Dessert – **Dessert**

Entrée – **First course**

Hors d'oeuvres – **Starter**

Menu du jour – **Today's menu**

Pâté maison – **Home made pâté**

En plus – **Extra (charge)**

Service à l'appréciation du client – **Service at the client's discretion**

Spécialité de la maison – **House speciality**

En sus – **Extra (charge)**

Varié – **Various/varied**

Déjeuner – **Lunch**

Dîner – **Evening meal**

Fromage – **Cheese**

Menu à la carte – **A la carte menu**

Menu à prix fixe – **Fixed price menu**

Plat du jour – **Dish of the day**

Prix nets – **Net price (no tip necessary)**

Service compris – **Service included**

Supplément (suppl.) – **Extra charge**

Tout compris – **Everything included**

Vin de maison – **House wine**

Interpreting the Items on a Menu

Here is a comprehensive list of dishes and culinary terms to help you to read menus:

A

abricot – **apricot**

ail – **garlic**

ananas – **pineapple**

agneau – **lamb**

allumettes (pommes) – **potato sticks**

andouille – **chitterling sausage**

à l'Anglaise – **steamed, boiled and served with butter**

armoricain – **creamy lobster sauce**

asperge – **asparagus**

assiette anglaise – **plate of cold cooked meats**

apéritif – **drink taken before a meal to aid appetite**

artichauts – **artichokes**

assiette – **plate**

avocat – **avocado**

B

baba au rhum – **rum baba (cake soaked in rum syrup)**

basquaise – **with sweet peppers, tomatoes and garlic**

betterave – **beetroot**

bien cuit – **well done**

bisque – **rich, creamy shellfish soup**

bleu – **(of steak) very rare, barely cooked**

Bleu de Bresse – **type of blue cheese**

boisson – **drink**

bouillabaisse – **fish stew**

boule – **a scoop of ice cream**

Brie – **type of soft cheese**

brioche – **cake with bread like texture**

baguette – **French stick (bread)**

beignet – **fritter**

beurre – **butter**

bifteck – **steak**

blanquette – **(stew) with cream added**

au bleu – **(of fish) cooked in stock with wine**

boeuf bourgignon – **Burgundy beef**

bon appétit! – **have a nice meal!**

bouillant – **boiling**

Boursin – **soft cheese with garlic and herbs**

(en) brochette – **on skewers**

Byrrh – **bitter sweet apéritif**

C

cabillaud – **cod**

cafetière – **coffee pot**

Calvados – **apple brandy**

canard – **duck**

carottes rapées – **grated carrots**

Carré de l'Est – **soft cheese**

casse-croûte – **a snack**

cassoulet – **stew made with beans, bacon and sausage**

chambré – **chilled**

charcuterie – **cold cooked meats**

chaud – **warm, hot**

(au) choix – **a choice of**

choucroute – **sauerkraut**

chou-fleur – **cauliflower**

citron – **lemon**

cocotte – **pot roast**

compôte de pommes – **stewed apple**

concombre – **cucumber**

confiture – **jam**

coq au vin – **chicken in red wine sauce**

côtelette – **cutlet**

cous-cous – **African stew served with semolina grain**

couvert – **place setting**

crème Anglaise – **custard**

Camembert – **soft cheese from Normandy**

carafe – **jug or bottle, usually one litre or half a litre**

carte des vins – **wine list**

cassis – **blackcurrant**

cerises – **cherries**

cervelles – **brains**

champignons – **mushrooms**

chasseur – **cooked in wine and cream**

chips – **potato crisps**

chou – **cabbage**

choux de Bruxelles – **Brussels sprouts**

citron pressé – **lemon squash**

coeur de céleri – **celery heart**

confit – **jellied**

casserole – **pan**

consommé – **clear soup**

contre-filet – **a cut of meat**

coquillages – **shellfish**

côte – **chop**

couteau – **knife**

couvert compris – **cover charge included**

Crème d'oeufs – **scrambled eggs**

crème caramel – **caramel cream dessert**

crêpe – **pancake**

crêperie – **pancake shop**

cresson – **water cress**

crevettes – **shrimps**

croissant – **crescent shaped breakfast roll**

croque-monsieur – **toasted cheese sandwich**

croque-madame – **toasted cheese sandwich with an egg on top**

croquettes – **rissoles, cro-quettes**

(en) croûte – **with a crust**

croûtons – **small pieces of bread crust**

crudités – **raw chopped vegetables in a vinaigrette dressing**

crustacés – **crabs, lobsters etc.**

cuiller/cuillère – **spoon**

cuisses de grenouille – **frogs' legs**

D

dégustation – **tasting**

déjeuner – **lunch**

demi – **half**

demi-sec – **medium dry**

digestif – **drink taken after a meal to aid digestion**

dinde, dindon – **turkey**

dîner – **evening meal**

duchesse (pommes) – **pota-toes mixed with egg yolks and browned**

doux – **sweet**

dur – **hard (hard boiled)**

E

eau de vie – **white brandy**

eau minérale – **mineral water**

échalottes – **shallots**

écrevisses – **crayfish**

Emmental – **type of cheese**

(à) emporter – **take-away**

entrée – **opening course, be-fore the main course**

entrecôte – **a cut of steak**

épaule – **shoulder**

escalope (de veau) – **thin slice (of veal)**

épinards – **spinach**

escargots – **snails**

F

farci – **stuffed**

fenouil – **fennel**

flambé – **flamed (in brandy or other liqueur)**

foie gras – **goose liver pâté**

frais – **fresh or chilled**

à la française – **boiled with lettuce and garlic**

fricassé – **fricasseed**

frites – **chips**

froid – **cold**

fruits de mer – **sea food/shell-fish**

faux-filet – **a cut of steak**

ficelle – **thin loaf of French bread**

foie – **liver**

fondu – **melted, a cheese dip**

fraise – **strawberry**

frappé – **ice cold**

frit(e) – **fried**

friture – **small fried fish**

fromage – **cheese**

fumé – **smoked**

G

galette – **type of cake/biscuit**

gâteau – **cake or tart**

gazeux – **fizzy**

glace – **ice, ice cream**

glaçon – **ice cube**

au gratin – **cooked with cheese**

grenadins – **medallions of veal**

grillé – **grilled**

garni – **garnished (often with vegetables)**

gauffre – **waffle**

gigot (d'agneau) – **leg (of lamb)**

glacé – **freezing cold**

goût – **taste**

(à la) Grecque – **cooked in an aromatic broth**

grenouille – **frog**

groseilles – **red currants**

H

hâché – **chopped up, minced**

hareng – **herring**

hollandaise – **egg and butter sauce**

hors d'oeuvres – **starter**

huîtres – **oysters**

hachis – **hash**

haricots verts – **green beans**

homard – **lobster**

huile (d'olive) – **(olive) oil**

J

jambon (cru) – **ham (raw)**

jardinière – **served with spring vegetables**

K

kirsch – **liqueur made from soft fruits**

L

laitue – **lettuce**

langoustine – **large prawn**

lapin – **rabbit**

lièvre – **hare**

Livarot – **a hard cheese**

lyonnaise – **cooked with onions**

langouste – **spiny lobster**

langue – **tongue**

légumes – **vegetables**

limande – **lemon sole**

lotte – **monkfish**

M

maison – **home-made**

marc – **(often homemade) liqueur or eau de vie (brandy)**

marrons – **chestnuts**

maquereau – **mackerel**

(à la) marinière – **boiled in white wine with onions**

marrons glacés – **candied fruits**

médaillon – **round or oval piece of meat**

merland – **whiting**

miel – **honey**

mirabelle – **small plum-like fruit**

moules – **mussels**

moutarde – **mustard**

mulet – **mullet**

merguez – **a spicy sausage**

meunière – **cooked with butter**

mille-feuille – **type of pastry/cake**

mornay – **served with a cheese sauce**

moules marinières – **mussels in a white wine sauce**

mouton – **mutton**

N

nature – **plain, unflavoured**

noisette – **nut**

nouilles – **noodles**

niçoise (salade) – **with olives, tomatoes and garlic**

noix de coco – **coco-nut**

O

oeuf (à la coque) – **(boiled) egg**

oeuf sur le plat – **fried egg**

oignons – **onions**

oeuf dur – **hard boiled egg**

oie – **goose**

P

pain – **bread**

parfum – **flavour**

parmentier – **contains potato**

pâtes – **pasta**

patron – **owner, proprietor**

persil – **parsley**

pamplemousse – **grapefruit**

parisienne – **in a white wine sauce**

pâté – **pâté (often made with livers)**

pâtisserie – **pastries**

pêche – **peach**

petit déjeuner – **breakfast**

petits gris – **type of snails**

pintade – **guinea fowl**

piquant – **spicy**

pistache – **pistachio nuts**

plateau – **tray**

à point – **medium (rare)**

poireau – **leek**

poitrine – **breast**

poivrons – **peppers (green/red)**

pomme de terre – **potato**

Pont L'Evêque – **a type of cheese**

portuguaise – **with tomato sauce**

pot au feu – **boiled beef and veg**

praline – **with ground almonds**

pruneaux – **prunes**

purée – **mashed**

petits pois – **peas**

pipérade – **Basque egg dish**

pissaladière – **olive and anchovy flan**

plat – **dish**

poché – **poached**

poire – **pear**

pois mangetout – **mangetout peas (you eat the pod as well)**

poivre – **pepper**

pomme – **apple**

(pommes) frites – **chips**

porc – **pork**

potage – **soup**

poulet – **chicken**

pritanier – **with spring vegetables**

prunes – **plums**

Q

quiche – **open tart made with cheese**

R

radis (au beurre) – **radish (in butter)**

raisins – **grapes**

ragoût – **stew**

raisin rhum – **rum and raisin**

ratatouille – **provençal vege-table stew with aubergines, peppers and garlic**

religieuse – **type of cake made with chou pastry**

rhum – **rum**

rillettes (de porc) – **potted pork**

riz – **rice**

rognons – **kidneys**

rosbif – **roast beef**

rôti – **roasted**

S

saignant – **rare (steak)**

Saint Paulin – **a semi-hard cheese**

salade – **usually just lettuce**

salé – **salted**

à votre santé! – **good health!**

sauce – **gravy, sauce**

sauce vinaigrette – **French dressing**

saucisson – **(salami type) sausage**

saumon (fumé) – **(smoked) salmon**

sautée (potatoes) – **sliced and fried in butter**

sec – **dry**

sel – **salt**

sorbet – **water ice, often served between courses**

soubise – **cream sauce with onions**

soucoupe – **saucer**

steak au poivre – **peppered steak**

sucré – **sugared**

en sus – **extra**

T

tarte aux pommes – **apple tart**

tartine – **piece of bread and butter (eaten at breakfast)**

tasse – **cup**

terrine – **potted meat like rough pâté**

thon – **tuna**

tournedos – **a cut of meat**

tranche – **slice**

truffe – **truffle, a type of underground mushroom used to flavour foods**

V

veau – **veal**

vapeur (potatoes) – **steamed/boiled**

verre – **glass**

viande – **meat**

vinaigrette – **salad dressing made with oil and wine vinegar**

vin rosé – **rosé wine**

volaille – **poultry**

vanille – **vanilla**

velouté de laitue – **cream of lettuce soup**

vert(e) (salade) – **green salad**

vinaigre – **vinegar**

vin blanc – **white wine**

vin rouge – **red wine**

Y

yaourt – **yoghurt**

What to say in a Restaurant

Have you a table for . . . people? – Vous avez une table pour . . . personnes?

There are four of us – Nous sommes quatre.

Waiter, please! – Monsieur (madame), s'il vous plaît!

Give me the menu, please – Donnez-moi le menu, s'il vous plaît.

Is there a special menu for children? – Il y a un menu spécial pour les enfants?

Give me the wine list – Donnez-moi la liste des vins.

The fixed-price menu, please – Le menu à prix fixe, s'il vous plaît.

The hundred franc menu – Le menu à cent francs.

The à la carte menu – Le menu à la carte.

What is the house speciality? – Quelle est la spécialité de la maison?

Have you any . . .? – Avez-vous des . . .?

I am ready to order – Je suis prêt à commander.

For starter I'll have . . . – Comme hors d'oeuvres je prendrai . . .

For main course I would like . . . – Comme plat du jour je voudrais . . .

For dessert give me . . . – Comme dessert donnez-moi . . .

What is the main course? – Qu'est-ce que c'est, le plat du jour?

What exactly is it? – Qu'est-ce que c'est exactement?

Is it hot or cold? – C'est chaud ou froid?

What have you got in the way of vegetables/ice creams/cheese? – Qu'est-ce que vous avez comme légumes/comme glaces/comme fromage?

Is there a choice of vegetables? – Il y a un choix de légumes?

What do you recommend in the way of . . .? – Qu'est-ce que vous recommandez comme . . .?

I would like the steak rare/medium/well done – Je voudrais le steak saignant/à point/bien cuit.

I would like a carafe (jug) of water – Je voudrais une carafe d'eau.

We are not having dessert – On ne prend pas le dessert.

A little/a lot – Un peu/beaucoup.

More bread/water/wine – Encore de pain/encore d'eau/encore de vin.

Pass me the salt/pepper – Passez-moi le sel/poivre.

With/without cream – Avec/sans crème.

Good health! – A votre santé!

Have a nice meal – Bon appétit.

Can I have a knife/fork/spoon/plate/glass? – Je peux avoir un couteau/une fourchette/une cuillère/une assiette/un verre?

This is not what I ordered – Ce n'est pas ce que j'ai commandé.

I did not order . . . – Je n'ai pas commandé . . .

The steak is not cooked enough – Le steak n'est pas assez cuit.

That smells nice – Ça sent bon.

It's delicious – C'est délicieux.

Give me the bill, please – Donnez-moi l'addition, s'il vous plaît.

I think there is a mistake – Je crois qu'il y a une erreur.

Is the service included? – Le service est compris?

I am in a rush – Je suis pressé.

The meal was excellent – Le repas était excellent.

N.B. Remember that if you are offered more of something and

you say *merci* (thank you), it means NO, THANK YOU. Say *Je veux bien* (I would like some) and *merci* only after you have received it.

Shopping,
Postal Services and Toilets

Shopping in France is an exciting experience. The novelty of seeing unusual products and familiar products in different packages takes away the drudgery. You can spend hours in a hypermarket comparing prices and studying the wonderful range of goods available.

The units of currency used in France are francs and centimes. There are a hundred centimes in a franc. Prices in the shops are usually shown as follows: 27,50 fr., which means 27 and a half francs. French shopkeepers understandably object to changing large notes when you only buy a postcard! Make sure you know what change to expect. Check it before you leave the shop. Arguing with a shopkeeper is a lost cause if you have left the shop before complaining.

La Boulangerie (Bakers)

From seven o'clock in the morning you can buy freshly baked bread, croissants and other pastries, often till seven or eight o'clock in the evenings and even on Sundays till noon. Bread is fairly cheap and very good on the day you buy it. The next day it becomes chewy and hard. You can revive it a little by toasting it. Croissants, which take their name from their crescent shape, are made from a mixture of puff pastry and bread. They are lovely when served straight from the oven. If you are staying on a campsite make sure you get to the shop early if you want croissants. They go like hot cakes! Your children will love *pains au chocolat* which are like croissants but have chocolate running through them. A *petit pain* is an ordinary bread roll.

La Pâtisserie (Cake shop)

One of the greatest pleasures of going to France is a visit to a *pâtisserie*. The selection of cakes, open fruit tarts and biscuits is marvellous. Although they are expensive they are a real treat.

La Charcuterie (Cooked meats shop or delicatessen)

You can buy many delicious things here – pâtés, hams, salami sausages, roast pork, vol au vents, roast chicken, prepared hors d'oeuvres, coleslaw, salads such as *salade niçoise*, pizzas and quiches. A truly French experience not to be missed!

Department Stores

Some of the better known stores are called Monoprix, Uniprix, Prisunic, Le Printemps, Les Galeries Lafayette and Nouvelles Galeries.

Supermarkets and Hypermarkets

Many of these are massive establishments with an impressive variety of goods and services. Some of the most well known are Rallye, Codec, Leclerc, Casino, Euromarché, Continent, Carrefour and Rondpoint.

Markets

You simply must find out when and where the local market takes place. There will almost certainly be one in the vicinity at least on Saturday mornings. Try to arrive early to see it at its best and expect it to close at about one o'clock. Shopping on a French market is a unique experience. The selection of fruit, vegetables, cheeses, herbs, cooked meats, hardware goods and clothes is wonderful.

Here is a list of shop names and departments in stores and supermarkets

alimentation – **food**

blanchisserie – **laundry**

boucherie chevaline – **horse meat butchers**

bricolage – **do it yourself**

charcuterie – **cooked meats shop**

comestibles – **food stuffs**

cordonnerie – **shoe repairs**

droguerie – **toiletries/hardware**

fromagerie – **cheese shop**

glacier – **ice cream shop**

jouets – **toys**

lessives – **washing powder/detergents**

magasin de cadeaux – **gift shop**

maison de la presse – **newspapers**

marchand de journaux – **newspapers**

marché – **market**

papeterie – **stationers**

pâtisserie – **cake shop**

pressing – **dry cleaners**

rayon (des disques) – **(record) department**

bijouterie – **jewellers**

boucherie – **butchers**

boutique – **small shop**

centre commercial – **shopping centre**

coiffeur/coiffeuse – **hair dresser**

confiserie – **sweet shop**

crémerie – **dairy shop**

épicerie – **grocers**

grand magasin – **department store**

hypermarché – **large supermarket**

journaux – **newspapers**

librairie – **book shop**

magasin de chaussures – **shoe shop**

marchand de fruits – **greengrocers**

marchand des vins – **wine merchants**

ménage – **household goods**

parfumerie – **perfume shop**

poissonnerie – **fishmongers**

quincaillerie – **hardware shop**

supermarché – **supermarket**

HYPERMARCHE
E.LECLERC

prisunic

SUPER U

surgelées – **frozen foods**

traiteur – **caterer/delicatessen**

vêtements – **clothes**

volailles – **poultry**

tabac – **tobacconists**

vaisselle – **crockery**

vins – **wines**

Shop Signs and What They Mean

accueil – **reception**

affaires du jour – **the day's bargains**

bon marché – **cheap**

cadeaux – **gifts**

chariots – **trolleys**

dames – **ladies' toilets**

dimanches et jours fériés – **Sundays and bank holidays**

entrée – **entrance**

entrée libre – **free entry**

escalier roulant – **escalator**

fermé – **closed**

gratuit – **free of charge**

hommes – **men's toilet**

interdit – **not allowed**

libre service – **self service**

ne pas se servir – **do not serve yourself**

occasion – **second hand**

ouvert – **open**

achats – **purchases**

ascenseur – **lift**

cabine d'essayage – **changing room**

caisse – **till, cash desk, checkout**

client suivant – **next customer**

défense de fumer – **no smoking**

à emporter – **take away**

entrée interdite – **no entry**

escalier – **stairs**

femmes – **women's toilets**

fermeture annuelle – **annual closing**

heures d'ouverture – **opening hours**

hors service – **out of order**

libre – **vacant**

à moitié prix – **half price**

ne pas toucher – **do not touch**

occupé – **engaged**

panier – **(supermarket) basket**

en panne – **broken down**

faites peser les légumes – **weigh your own vegetables**

poussez – **push**

prêt à porter – **ready to wear**

prix – **price**

prix réduits – **reduced prices**

faire la queue – **queue up**

réclamations – **complaints**

rez-de-chaussée – **ground floor**

servez-vous – **serve yourself**

soldes – **sale (reduced prices)**

sortie sans achat – **exit for those who have bought nothing**

tirez – **pull**

à vendre – **for sale**

veuillez présenter vos sacs vides aux caisses – **please allow your empty bags to be inspected**

à partir de – **from (one price to another)**

plats cuisinés – **cooked dishes**

premier étage – **first floor**

privé – **private**

prix choc – **bargains**

promotion – **special offer**

rayon – **section/department**

réclame – **advertisement**

salon d'essayage – **changing room**

service après vente – **after-sales service**

sortie (de secours) – **(emergency) exit**

sous-sol – **basement**

T.V.A. – **value added tax (V.A.T.)**

vente – **(for) sale**

♦ *What to take with you and not to buy in France*

In our experience you will save money by taking with you the follow goods:

tea or tea bags

instant coffee

cordials

sauces

sugar
packet soups
jam/marmalade
salt and pepper
rice and pasta
cooking oil
baby foods
cleaning materials
toilet tissues
paper tissues

biscuits
sweets
cereals
tins of meat
toiletries
sun tan cream
baked beans
films
kitchen rolls

♦ *Items to bring home from France*

Cheeses – over five hundred kinds to choose from
Pâté
Mustard – *Moutarde de Dijon* is very good
Spices and herbs – Mixed Provence herbs are excellent
Liqueur chocolates
Marinated fruits
Bars of chocolate from supermarkets
Le Creuset pans – very heavy and good quality
Kitchen utensils – supermarkets have a superb range
Wine – the best selection in the world
Packs of beer – very good value for money
Local spirits and liqueurs
Coffee – please note that *grains* are beans. If you want ground
coffee you look for the word *moulu* on the packet
Drinking chocolate
Glassware
Breakfast coffee bowls
Soufflé dishes
Brioche tins
Pâté dishes
Postcards and slides as souvenirs of places visited
C.D.s – shop around in large supermarkets.

What to say in a shop
What the shopkeeper might say to you

Qu'y a-t-il pour votre service? – **What can I do for you?**
Vous désirez? – **What would you like?**
Je peux vous aider? – **Can I help you?**
Combien en voulez-vous? – **How much/how many do you want?**
Et avec ça? – **Anything else?**
C'est tout? – **Is that all?**
Voilà – **There you are.**
Je n'en ai plus – **I have none left.**
C'est pour offrir? – **Is it for a present?**
C'est quelle taille? – **What size (clothes)?**
C'est quelle pointure? – **What size (shoes)?**
Avez-vous de la monnaie? – **Have you any change?**
Ça va? – **Is that okay?**
Vous payez en liquide? – **Are you paying cash?**
Vous payez à la caisse – **You pay at the till/checkout**

Ways of asking for things

I would like . . . – Je voudrais . . .
I want . . . – Je veux . . .
Give me . . . – Donnez-moi . . .
I'll have that – Je prends ça.
I'll have two of them – J'en prendrai deux.
I need – Il me faut/J'ai besoin de
Have you any . . .? – Avez-vous des . . .?
Do you sell . . .? – Vous vendez . . .?
What have you got in the way of . . .? – Qu'est-ce que vous avez comme . . .?
I prefer that – Je préfère ça.
Give me a piece like that – Donnez-moi un morceau comme ça.
Can I try it on? – Je peux l'essayer?
Can I listen to this record? – Je peux écouter ce disque?
Can I taste this cheese? – Je peux goûter ce fromage?

Can I look at those shoes? – Je peux voir ces chaussures?

Have you these shoes in a size 38? – Vous avez ces chaussures en trente-huit?

I would like to spend about a hundred francs – Je voudrais dépenser environ cent francs.

I'm looking for something for (my father) – Je cherche quelque chose pour (mon père).

Do you have it in white (blue, green)? – Vous l'avez en blanc (bleu, vert)?

Have you nothing else? – Vous n'avez pas autre chose?

Have you anything cheaper? – Avez-vous quelque chose de moins cher?

Have you anything bigger/smaller? – Avez-vous quelque chose de plus grand/plus petit?

It's for a present – C'est pour offrir.

Can you wrap it? – Pouvez-vous l'envelopper?

Can you gift wrap it for me? – Pouvez-vous me faire un paquet cadeau?

I'm just looking – Je regarde seulement.

No, I don't like it – Non, je ne l'aime pas.

It's too big, small, long, short – C'est trop grand, petit, long, court.

How much do I need to buy?

A kilo of – Un kilo de, **Half a kilo of** – Un demi-kilo de

A pound of – Une livre de, **500 grammes of** – Cinq cent grammes de

200 grammes of – deux cent grammes de, **A litre of** – Un litre de

Half a litre of – Un demi-litre de, **A bottle of** – Une bouteille de

A carafe (jug) of – Une carafe de, **A box/tin of** – Une boîte de

A sachet of – Un sachet de, **A slice of** – Une tranche de

A piece of – Un morceau de, **A portion of** – Une portion de

A packet of – Un paquet de, **A pot of** – Un pot de

A bag of – Un sac de, **A jar of** – Un bocal de

A bar of – Une tablette de, **A (small perfume type) bottle of** – Un flacon de

Finding your way around a large store

Excuse me, is there a . . . near here? – Excusez-moi, il y a un . . . près d'ici?
Where is the record department? – Où est le rayon des disques?
Where is the changing room? – Où est le salon d'essayage?
Where are the toilets? – Où sont les toilettes?
What floor is it on? – C'est à quel étage?

Paying

That's all thank you – C'est tout merci.
How much is it? – C'est combien?
What is the price? – Quel est le prix?
How much is that altogether? – C'est combien en tout?
It's too dear – C'est trop cher.
Can you change a hundred franc note? – Pouvez-vous changer un billet de cent francs?
Have you got change for a hundred francs? – Vous avez la monnaie de cent francs?
I'm sorry, I have no change – Je regrette, je n'ai pas de monnaie.
Here is a fifty franc/a hundred franc note – Voici un billet de cinquante/de cent francs.
Do you accept travellers' cheques/eurocheques? – Vous acceptez des chèques de voyages/des eurochèques?

Complaining

I am not satisfied – Je ne suis pas satisfait.
Please can I have my money back? – Voulez-vous me rembourser, s'il vous plaît.
Will you exchange it for another one? – Voulez-vous l'échanger pour un autre?
Will you check the change, please, I think there is a mistake?

– Voulez-vous vérifier la monnaie, s'il vous plaît, je crois qu'il y a une erreur?

♦ *Using Postal Services*

In France you can buy stamps either at the post office or at the tobacconist's – *bureau de tabac*, which is easily identified by the red cigar-shaped sign displayed outside. The Post Office – *la Poste* has the abbreviation P.T.T. – *Postes, Télégraphes, Téléphones* or P&T – *Postes et Télécommunications*. Near busy post offices you may also find yellow stamp machines – *distributeurs automatiques*. Book shops and stationers' which sell postcards will normally sell you stamps, but only for the postcards you have bought.

Post offices are open on weekdays from eight o'clock to twelve noon and from two till seven in the evening. On Saturdays they close at noon. It costs slightly more to send a letter to the United Kingdom than a postcard. If you wish to send a parcel to Britain you will be asked to fill in a small green self-adhesive customs label on which you declare the contents of the parcel. You can also buy at the post office special parcel boxes *emballages préformés* which are strong and reliable. French post boxes are quite small and yellow in colour. They are usually fixed onto walls near post offices and tobacconists. On them are displayed the times of collections and a warning that you should not post newspapers and printed matter in the box. If you are in Paris the box is likely to have two slots labelled *PARIS EXCLUSIVEMENT* for local mail, and *AUTRES DIRECTIONS* for destinations outside Paris. Sometimes there may be a third slot labelled *L'ETRANGER* for letters whose destination is outside France.

If you are expecting to receive mail at your address in France you may be disappointed by the length of time taken for it to arrive. French postal services are often disrupted at holiday times because many postal workers are themselves on holiday. Remember also that if letters from Great Britain are understamped they may not be delivered at all.

If you are touring and have no fixed address you can take

advantage of the *Poste Restante* service. For a small charge letters addressed to you *Poste Restante* will be held at the post office for you until you claim them by producing some form of identification.

Telephones

In France there are 167,000 public telephones. It is cheaper to make calls between nine thirty p.m. and eight a.m. on weekdays and between two p.m. on Saturday and eight a.m. on Monday. Calls can also be made on cheap rate during public holidays.

In a coin operated telephone box you pick up the receiver and put in your coins. It is best to use five franc coins which you can collect from your change when shopping. The coins drop behind a glass screen and will be visible. The value of the coins inserted will be displayed. Next you should dial 00 and wait for a tone. Dial 44 and then the United Kingdom STD code minus the leading zero and finally your correspondent's number. The ringing tone in France sounds rather like our engaged signal with longer pips. The engaged signal is a series of pips a little more rapid than in Britain. If you finish your conversation before your money runs out, the coins still visible will be returned to you automatically when you put down the receiver.

Here is an example, with translation, of the dialling instructions for making a call to Britain:

DÉCROCHEZ LE COMBINÉ – **Lift the receiver**

INTRODUISEZ DES PIÈCES – **Put in some coins**

ATTENDEZ LA TONALITÉ – **Wait for the tone**

COMPOSEZ L'INDICATIF DU PAYS (44) – **Dial the country code (44)**

COMPOSEZ L'INDICATIF DE LA ZONE AUTOMAT-IQUE (EN SUPPRIMANT LA PREMIER 0) – **Dial the area code minus the leading zero**

COMPOSEZ LE NUMÉRO – **Dial the number**

EN CAS DE NON RÉPONSE, RACCROCHEZ LE COMBINÉ ET VOS PIÈCES SERONT RESTITUÉS – **Put down the receiver and your coins will be returned to you**

EN CAS DE DIFFICULTÉ, APPUYEZ SUR LE BOUTON

LA POSTE ➤

Enseigne d'un bureau de poste.
Post Office sign.
Schild eines Postamts.
Insegna di un ufficio postale.
Letrero de una oficina de correos.
Uithangbord voor postkantoor.

Boîte aux lettres.
Letterbox.
Briefkasten.
Cassetta per le lettere.
Buzón de correos.
Brievenbus.

Cabine téléphonique.
Telephone booth.
Fernsprechzelle.
Cabina telefonica.
Cabina telefónica.
Telefooncel.

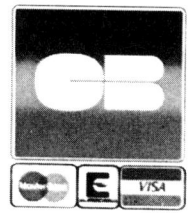 

ET RECOMMENCEZ L'OPÉRATION – **In case of difficulty, press the button and start the operation again.**

Card Phones

There are now a large number of card phones available (usually when you want a coin operated one!). In order to use these you need a **Télécarte** which can be bought in post offices and railway stations. Cards are sold in units of 50 and 120. If you intend to make several calls to the United Kingdom it may be a good investment. Télécartes are very easy to use. Just follow these instructions:

DÉCROCHEZ – **Lift the receiver**
INTRODUIRE CARTE – **Put in your card**
PATIENTEZ, S'IL VOUS PLAÎT – **Hold on please**
CRÉDIT (20) UNITÉS – **(20) units left**
NUMÉROTEZ – **Dial the number**
NUMÉRO APPELÉ – **Number called**
RACCROCHEZ – **Put receiver down**
RETIREZ VOTRE CARTE – **Take out your card**

It is still possible to make telephone calls from the post office. You should find the counter which deals with telephone calls. The clerk will direct you to a booth and will usually dial the number for you. You pay for the call afterwards. If you ask for a person to person call the charge is likely to be double and will begin when you speak to the named person. It is also very tempting to telephone from your hotel or from the local café or restaurant. Please bear in mind that you may be charged up to 40% more for this service.

What to say when using postal services

How do I get to the post office? – Pour aller à la poste?
What time does the post office open? – La poste ouvre à quelle heure?
How much is it to send . . .? – C'est combien pour envoyer . . .?

I would like to send . . . – Je voudrais envoyer . . .
A letter to England – Une lettre en Angleterre.
A postcard to Scotland – Une carte postale en Ecosse.
A parcel to Wales – Un paquet au Pays de Galles.
I would like a two franc thirty stamp – Je voudrais un timbre à deux francs trente.
A stamp for Great Britain – Un timbre pour la Grande Bretagne.
Where is the letter box? – Où est la boîte aux lettres?
Is there a telephone box near here? – Il y a une cabine téléphonique près d'ici?
Have you a telephone? – Avez-vous le téléphone?
Can I telephone from here? – Je peux téléphoner d'ici?
I'd like to telephone England. Can you tell me how to do it? – Je voudrais téléphoner en Angleterre. Comment ça se fait?
Can I make a call and reverse the charges? – Je peux faire un P.C.V.?
I would like to make a person to person call – Je voudrais un préavis personnel.
Have you any five franc coins? – Avez-vous des pièces de cinq francs?

♦ *French Toilets*

The rumours you have heard that some French toilets are revolting are largely true! Some have been so smelly that we have come out with our legs still crossed. Also public toilets are sometimes difficult to find. If you are desperate and cannot find a public toilet, walk into a bar or café, use the toilets and walk out again. Petrol stations, department stores and public buildings have them too.

Not all toilets are horrible, far from it. Many are supervised and kept very clean by an attendant, usually an elderly person, who may charge you a franc or expect a small tip. It is worth it!

Some French toilets are the so called *Turque* type hole in the ground, which look rather like a shower base with a round hole in the middle and two platforms for your feet. On some campsites we have seen a row of these with one normal toilet cubicle at the

end of the row. Guess where all the English people queue up even when all the others are vacant! One word of warning, if you do use the *Turque* type toilet, step out quickly when you flush, otherwise your feet will be soaked by the splashing water.

If you cannot find any toilets at all you can always go into a field behind a clump of trees. French men do not even bother with the trees. They just go to the toilet at the roadside. When you pass them on the road they are not standing there admiring the view! If you do go into a field please do not stand on an ant hill like I once did or you will come out of the field suffering from Saint Vitus' Dance! When in France, always take a good supply of toilet paper with you. You will rarely find any in public toilets.

What to say if you need a toilet

Is there a public toilet near here? – Il y a une toilette publique près d'ici?
Where is the toilet, please? – Où est la toilette, s'il vous plaît?

Santé

Ambulances

TAXI AMBULANCE

Philippe RACINE

SUR APPEL 24 H/24
Toutes Distances
Taxis jusqu'à 6 Personnes

51 39 40 80

9, rue Pierre Mandin
85740 L'EPINE

AMBULANCES ✳

RENOUX Marc
TAXIS

4 et 6 Passagers

51 39 75 75

VSL - AMBULANCE

Toutes Distances
Permanence Téléphonique

24 H / 24

Véhicules Climatisés

Transport de Corps
avant mise en bière
Impasse de la Cloison
85680 LA GUERINIERE
NOIRMOUTIER

Pharmacies

__BARBATRE__
PERIER Solange Pl du Marché   5139 3848
__L'EPINE__
SOETE René 6 Av Liberté   5139 3045
__LA GUERINIERE__
ARTAUX Michel 2 R Centrale   5139 8151
__NOIRMOUTIER__
GIRAUD 2 R Janvier   5139 0026
RAIMONDEAU Thérèse
10 R Marié Lemonnier   5139 2355
SERVANT 21 Grande Rue   5139 1337

Médecins

URGENCES MEDICALES
Faites le 15

__BARBATRE__
PERIER Gilles
Chem Barre Raguideau   5139 6685
__L'EPINE__
DRIE Françoise
4 R Gal Charette   5139 1636
__LA GUERINIERE__
PEIGNE Bertrand
6 R Pierre Monnier   5139 6543
__NOIRMOUTIER__
AUDEON Jacky
24 R Prée au Duc   5139 1140
DRIE Françoise
26 Rue Menisiére   5139 0745
FEVRE Bernard
2 R Liniére   5139 0564
FREUDIGER Alain
25 R Joseph Pineau   5139 3703
GUICHERD Alain
1 R Richer   5139 1058
GUILLOTIN William
24 R Prée au Duc   5139 1140
VERRIER Marie-Claude
24 R Prée au Duc   5139 1140
MEDECINE DU TRAVAIL
Place de la Mairie
LA GUERINIERE   5139 8585
Avenue de la Victoire
NOIRMOUTIER   5139 8820

Illness

There is always the possibility that you or a member of your family will become ill or have an accident while you are in France. You would not think twice about going to the doctor's dentist's or chemist's in Britain, but you might feel very apprehensive if the situation arises in France. There are, however, certain measures you can take to help you to cope, particularly with the financial implications.

You will find that brand names of pharmaceutical goods are different, so where possible it is best to take them with you in a first-aid kit, containing at least the following basic items:

first-aid booklet	aspirin
Diocalm or Arret	thermometer
throat lozenges	antiseptic cream
plasters	bicarbonate of soda
Wasp-Eze	bandages
calamine lotion	insect bite cream
elastic bandage	cough linctus
sunburn cream	cotton wool
indigestion tablets	Optrex
sterile dressing	cold remedies
vaseline	gauze
decongestant capsules	tweezers
safety pins	travel sickness pills
scissors	

Preventative Measures

You will have heard of the so-called 'continental tummy'. Upset stomachs can be caused by numerous factors, not least the tension and excitement of going on holiday. A series of simple precautions can minimise the problem. It may be a good idea to avoid drinking tap water especially on campsites, although we have always found it to be safe. Avoid taps where the notice *EAU NON POTABLE* is displayed. Bottled water is cheap when bought in a supermarket in large bottles and it aids digestion.

Try to avoid eating large amounts of oily or spicy foods. Green salads in France, for example, are often served with an oily dressing. Be careful with seafood. Raw vegetables, salads and unpeeled fruit; raw shellfish; cream, ice cream and ice cubes; underdone meat or fish, and uncooked, cold or reheated food generally can all be contaminated. Freshly cooked foods are safer. The same comments could, of course, be made about food in this country. The irresistible attraction of a wide variety of cheap wines and exciting liqueurs and the *ambiance* of your campsite may influence you into drinking more than you are used to. The resulting hangover will be very unpleasant.

If a member of your family has a known illness or needs regular medication, say for hay fever, make sure that you have enough supplies to last until the end of the holiday. It would be very difficult and potentially dangerous for a French doctor to pre-scribe drugs when he is unaware of your medical history. Bear in mind also that glass bottles are liable to break. It is no use taking adequate supplies of medicine only to find the bottles broken in your luggage.

The Chemist

You should be aware of the rôle of the chemist in France. The cost of consultations with doctors is quite high, so the French use chemists much more than we do to ask for advice about the treatment of minor ailments. If the illness in question needs the attention of a doctor the chemist will advise you accordingly. Chemists are usually very helpful and they will treat minor cuts and bruises. In France the chemist's is the only place you can buy medicines and drugs, even aspirin. A chemist's can be recognised by the green cross displayed outside or a symbol of two snakes entwined round a staff. If the chemist's is closed you will see a notice on the door telling you where the nearest open one is. It is called a *Pharmacie de Garde.*

E111 Certificate

Your E111 certificate is a very important document. It entitles you to the same medical care as French people. They have to pay for consultations, medicines and treatment. It is expensive, but they can reclaim about eighty per cent of the cost of a consultation and between seventy and ninety per cent for medicines. It is more expensive for a doctor to visit you than if you can make it to the surgery. With your E111 there will be detailed information about the procedure for going to the doctor's and for reclaiming medical expenses. Normally the doctor will give you a *Feuille de Soins* which serves as a receipt for the money you have paid for the consultation. When you pay for your prescription, which is on the same document, you should keep the *Vignette* (self-adhesvie price label). Remove it from the packet or bottle and stick it to the prescription form. You will need it in order to claim from the social security.

If you have a serious illness or an accident involving hospitalisation, although your E111 will help you to reclaim a large proportion of your expenses, even ten per cent of the cost of prolonged treatment or hospital bills is certain to amount to a substantial sum of money. In order to cover this contingency you would be well advised to take out a holiday insurance policy which covers medical expenses. The motoring organisations and the Caravan Club include this kind of cover in their policies.

Rabies

Finally, you can contract rabies if you are bitten, scratched or even licked by an infected dog, cat, fox or other animal. It is wise to avoid stroking or feeding dogs and cats, no matter how cuddly and friendly they seem. If you are bitten or scratched whilst abroad, you should wash the wound immediately with soap and clean water and get medical attention fast. You may need a rabies vaccination. The French word for rabies is *la Rage*.

What to say when you are ill

Can you help me please? – Pouvez-vous m'aider, s'il vous plaît?
I need a doctor/dentist – J'ai besoin d'un médecin/dentiste.
Is it possible to see the doctor? – Je voudrais voir le médecin, c'est possible?
Can I have an appointment to see the doctor/dentist? – Je peux avoir un rendez-vous avec le médecin/dentiste?
It's urgent – C'est urgent.
As soon as possible – Le plus tôt possible.
I've been ill for (two days) – Je souffre depuis (deux jours).
I am worried about my wife/husband/son/daughter – Je suis inquiet au sujet de ma femme/mon mari/mon fils/ma fille.
Can you recommend something for insect bites/a burn/sunstroke? – Pouvez-vous me conseiller quelque chose contre une piqûre/une brûlure/un coup de soleil?
Can you recommend some medication? – Pouvez-vous me conseiller un médicament?
Can you give me a prescription? – Pouvez-vous me donner une ordonnance?
Is there a hospital near here? – Il y a un hôpital près d'ici?
Can you give me a receipt? – Pouvez-vous me donner un reçu?
Is there a chemist's near here? – Il y a une pharmacie près d'ici?
Will you make up this prescription for me? – Voulez-vous me préparer cette ordonnance?
I am better, thank you – Ça va mieux, merci.

How to describe symptoms

I am ill – Je suis malade.
I do not feel well – Je ne me sens pas très bien.

My wife, husband, son, daughter is ill – Ma femme, mon mari, mon fils, ma fille est malade.

I feel really bad – J'ai vraiment mal.

I have a headache – J'ai mal à la tête.

I have a sore eye – J'ai mal à l'oeil.

I have sore eyes – J'ai mal aux yeux.

I have a sore ear/earache – J'ai mal à l'oreille.

I have sore ears – J'ai mal aux oreilles.

I have stomach ache – J'ai mal au ventre.

I have a sore knee – J'ai mal au genou.

I have hurt my shoulder, arm, hand, finger – Je me suis fait mal à l'épaule, au bras, à la main, au doigt.

I have hurt my back, leg, foot – Je me suis fait mal au dos, à la jambe, au pied.

I am very tired – Je suis très fatigué.

I have a migraine – J'ai une migraine.

I have hay fever – J'ai un rhume des foins.

I am constipated – Je suis constipé.

I have diarrhoea – J'ai la diarrhée.

I am cold – J'ai froid.

I am hot – J'ai chaud.

I feel dizzy – J'ai la tête qui tourne.

I cannot breathe – Je ne peux pas respirer.

I cannot eat – Je ne peux pas manger.

I have no appetite – Je n'ai pas d'appétit.

I cannot sleep – Je ne peux pas dormir.

I cannot swallow – Je ne peux pas avaler.

I have an inflamed throat – J'ai la gorge enflammée.

I feel that I am going to be sick – J'ai envie de vomir.

I feel sick – J'ai mal au coeur.

I have been sick three times – J'ai vomi trois fois.

I am full of a cold – Je suis enrhumé.

I have a temperature – J'ai de la fièvre.

I have an allergy – J'ai une allergie.

I have indigestion – J'ai une indigestion.

I have sunstroke – J'ai un coup de soleil.

I think I have caught flu – Je crois que j'ai attrapé la grippe.

I am coughing a lot – Je tousse beaucoup.

I cannot stop coughing – Je n'arrête pas de tousser.
I have broken my arm – Je me suis cassé le bras.
I have cut my hand – Je me suis coupé la main.
I have burned my fingers – Je me suis brûlé les doigts.
I have injured my leg – Je me suis blessé la jambe.
I have trapped a finger – Je me suis coincé un doigt.
I have sprained my ankle – Je me suis foulé la cheville.
I have a pain here – J'ai une douleur ici.
I have tooth-ache – J'ai mal aux dents.
I have lost a filling – J'ai perdu un plombage.

Some useful medical words

ointment – la pommade, **aspirin** – l'aspirine
pills – des pilules, **pastilles** – des pastilles
lotion – une lotion, **cream** – une crème
disinfectant – un désinfectant, **dressing** – un pansement
sticking plaster – un sparadrap, **cotton wool** – du coton hydro-phile
cough medicine – du sirop contre la toux, **tablets** – des cachets
tablets – des comprimés, **drops** – des gouttes
antiseptic – antiseptique, **a remedy** – un remède
medicine – un médicament

Suggested Activities for the Children

Children can gain a great deal of knowledge and enjoyment by using their holiday as a learning experience. The following ideas will give the holiday an educational purpose and an extra dimension. If you are studying French at school remember that a good general knowledge about France will help you to cope with the National Curriculum.

1. Persuade your parents to buy you cheap road maps of Britain and France. Mark the route as you travel.
2. Impress your French teacher by writing a letter to the tourist office asking for a plan of the town and general information. You will be thrilled when you receive a reply.
3. Write a diary of your visit and make a scrapbook when you arrive home. It will give you pleasure in later years.
4. Make a collection of coins, transport and entertainment tickets, brochures, supermarket bills, labels and wrappers, newspapers, magazines, postcards and menus.
5. See how many of these shops you can spot. Tick them off.

bijouterie	boucherie	charcuterie	coiffeur	confiserie
cordonnerie	crémerie	droguerie	épicerie	glacier
librairie	maison de la presse	papeterie	pâtisserie	poissonnerie
pressing	quincaillerie	tabac		

6. Buy a telephone card and try making a call to Britain.

7. Write a list of all the ice cream flavours you can find. Try all the flavours you don't know!

8. Ask your parents to let you do the food shopping. It is easier than you think.

9. Force your parents to speak French in the car! Try car registration plates to practise your numbers. Use the chapter in this book to find everyday phrases. Try building conversation dialogues gradually. Put yourself into imaginary situations.

10. Buy a television magazine and see how many of the programmes you can recognise.

11. Start a vocabulary book. Write in it all the phrases you think you will need and add to the list as you learn new words and phrases.

12. Try to make friends with children of your own age. Kick your ball near their tent and thank them when they return it! Offer them sweets, show them your comics, persuade your parents to invite their parents for an aperitif. Try any ploy you can, but talk to them! Why not ask for their addresses so that you can start a correspondence with them.

13. Pubs in Britain often have quaint or unusual names. So do French cafés and restaurants. Make a list of all the interesting names you see and find out what they mean in English.

14. Write down a menu you have tried. Show the name of the restaurant, the prices, the service charge and any other useful information. Use the menu on page 140.

15. Look for these items in a supermarket or shop. Write down the weight (where appropriate) and the French price. When you come back to Britain compare the prices.

Item	Amount	French price	English price
lemonade			
chocolate			
bread			
cheap wine			
ice cream			
butter			
sugar			
apples			
potatoes			
training shoes			
jeans			
pullover			
tights			
book			
compact disc			
cassette			
petrol			

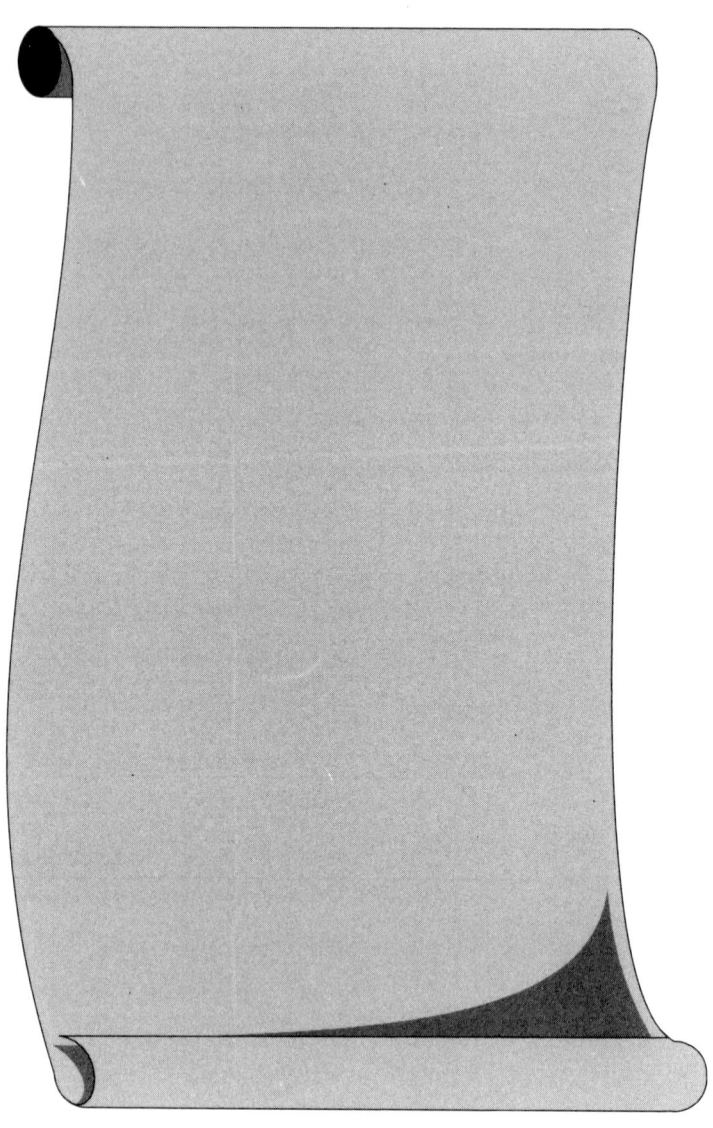

16. See if you can spot the following things and take a close look at them. In what ways are they different?

A 'turque' type toilet	Road markings	How windows close
A bidet	A policeman	Shutters on windows
A fire engine	Electric sockets	An ambulance
What houses are built of	Gardens	Floors in houses
Sink plugs	How the French greet each other	

17. Have your photo taken in front of typically French places – a post box, a bus stop, unusual shops, the town hall or a market stall.
18. Take a small battery operated cassette recorder with you. Try to record snippets of conversation and the sounds on the market or in a restaurant.
19. How many of these quiz questions can you answer?

    a. How far is a kilometre in miles?
    b. Why does a French bus have two passenger doors?
    c. What happens at a roundabout?
    d. Describe the sequence of traffic lights.
    e. Name three types of French cheese.
    f. How many makes of French car can you find?
    g. What is lead-free petrol called in French?
    h. What colour is a post box?
    i. Name three different supermarkets.
    j. What does it say on shop doors for 'push' and 'pull'?
    k. What is an 'auto-école'?
    l. Where would you see the initials B.N.P.?
    m. What is a 'zone bleue'?
    n. How much is a litre of petrol?
    o. Who would be taller, a man of six feet or a man of two metres?
    p. How much does it cost to send a postcard to Britain?

q. What is a 'barbe à papa'? What does the phrase mean in English?

r. What is the French for 'frogs' legs'?

s. Where would you find a red, cigar-shaped sign?

t. What are 'baguettes' and 'ficelles'?

u. How many different French coins are there?

v. What is 'le Shuttle'?

w. What colours are the French flag (in the right order from the flagpole) and what is its popular name?

x. Who works in a 'commissariat'?

y. What do the letters S.N.C.F. stand for?

z. How much does a telephone card cost?

(Fill in answers below)

a.	n.
b.	o.
c.	p.
d.	q.
e.	r.
f.	s.
g.	t.
h.	u.
i.	v.
j.	w.
k.	x.
l.	y.
m.	z.

20. Can you find six drinks in this word snake? The section on buying a drink will help.

21. Make up another word snake using the words for various fruits and vegetables.

22. Match up the following pairs to make ten places you would find in a town. The section on Finding Your Way Around will help.

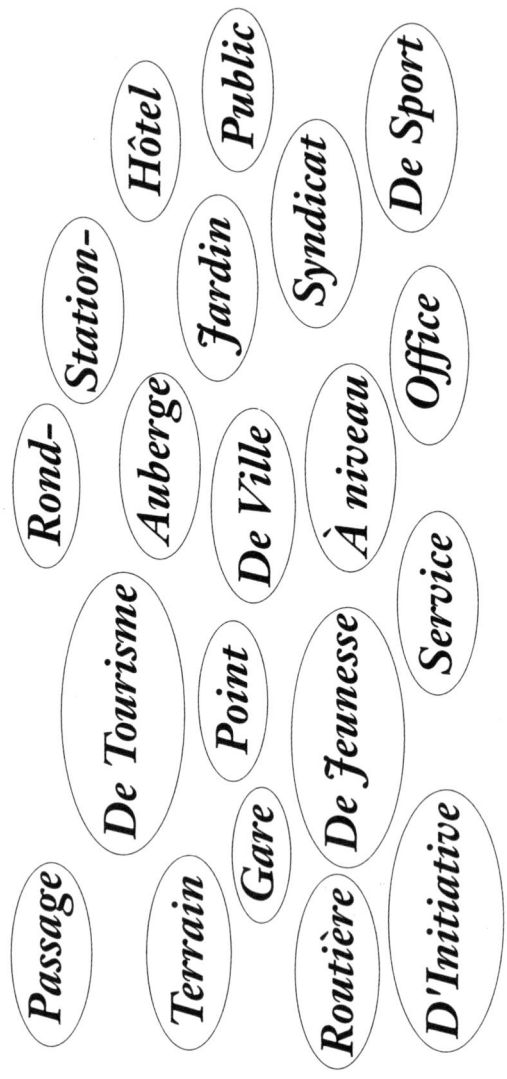

23. Drinks wordsearch.

These 20 drinks are hidden in this wordsearch. Can you find them?

Eau minérale, bière, cidre, lait, apéritif, tisane, thé
citron, café, crème, Cognac, coca-cola, pastis, chocolat
pamplemousse, Pernod, orange, Suze, vin rouge, Chartreuse

```
C  H  O  C  O  L  A  T  A  B  D  F  H  T  H  E
F  E  C  A  Z  S  X  W  U  S  Q  P  N  L  K  I
G  H  J  L  M  S  U  T  A  P  E  R  N  O  D  G
A  L  C  F  A  P  B  Z  O  C  U  D  V  N  E  W
F  R  A  Q  G  V  G  H  E  W  G  J  Y  E  K  C
C  S  F  P  Z  W  U  M  V  T  X  H  R  F  Z  I
O  M  E  B  E  N  E  C  O  P  O  D  Q  D  R  T
C  T  Y  L  X  R  M  A  W  N  I  U  O  C  E  R
A  P  I  Q  C  S  I  T  S  C  F  R  A  H  B  O
C  H  C  X  O  D  Y  T  V  T  E  I  E  A  S  N
O  R  A  N  G  E  H  Z  I  L  B  U  D  R  T  M
L  N  J  P  N  Q  S  R  G  F  T  Q  U  T  R  A
A  F  B  P  A  S  T  I  S  B  C  F  C  R  D  L
E  A  F  G  C  H  B  C  T  I  S  A  N  E  Q  F
V  I  N  R  O  U  G  E  G  E  K  E  J  U  I  K
L  J  M  N  Y  D  O  D  E  R  K  P  R  S  O  P
X  Z  K  E  A  U  M  I  N  E  R  A  L  E  A  L
K  A  D  F  C  G  J  M  H  B  I  X  J  O  N  A
F  X  L  T  M  L  S  M  F  A  N  D  S  T  Y  I
P  A  M  P  L  E  M  O  U  S  S  E  A  Z  A  T
```

Tips in Brief

1. Rabies can kill. Do not stroke animals. If you are scratched or bitten get treatment immediately. Do not take your pet abroad. Quarantine laws will separate you from your pet for six months on your return.
2. French toilets often have no toilet paper. Have some with you all the time.
3. Do not forget your E111 certificate. You will have to produce it if you see a doctor or go to hospital.
4. Make sure you have a bottle opener! The wine is too good to miss!
5. Take a spare car (caravan) key with you and keep it separate from the other.
6. In 'hole in the ground' (*Turque* type) toilets move your feet quickly when you flush!
7. Take a continental mains adaptor with you so that you can use a hairdryer, shaver, electric rollers, cassette player.
8. French people have little time for British tourists who do not try to speak at least a little French.
9. Lead-free petrol is now widely available.
10. Electricity on campsites is often only five amps. An electric kettle will blow a fuse. You can often choose what ampage you want.
11. Do not put English stamps on your postcards!
12. In a café drinks can be slightly cheaper at the bar than at the table.
13. French people are very polite to each other. They appreciate *s'il vous plaît* and *merci*. A handshake is always appreciated, every day if you make friends.
14. A *librairie* is a bookshop not a library.

15. If you ask for *une bière* you will probably get bottled beer. *Un demi* will get you a glass of draught.
16. Police will fine you on the spot for motoring offences.
17. Put your headlights on in tunnels and in poor visibility.
18. Banks can sometimes be closed on Mondays.
19. A letter C on a tap means HOT (*chaud*). Warn the children!
20. At a controlled crossing, only cross on green. The police are very strict.
21. Look for menus with *service compris* if you do not want to leave a tip.
22. You are subject to the laws of the country. It is in your interests not to break them.
23. If an emergency leaves you without money and banks are closed, the British Consulate will help you to contact relatives in order to transfer funds.
24. Tourists, and more particularly caravaners, are vulnerable to robbers on the open road and in lay-bys. Be alert to the dangers.
25. Keep an eye on the exchange rate in your newspaper. Change your money when the rate is favourable.
26. Do not buy duty free wine on the boat. There is a much better choice at more favourable prices in supermarkets.
27. Beware of the alcohol volume stated on bottles of spirits. 20% volume (on the Guy Lussac scale of measurement) is roughly equivalent to 70% proof.
28. Caravaners requiring an electrical hook-up should take a continental adaptor, available from your caravan shop. Hook-ups on some sites are the same as ours.
29. On arrival at hotels, campsites and youth hostels, you will be asked to fill in a *Fiche de Voyageur*, which contains your personal and passport details and the date you entered France.
30. In a busy town the best time to find a parking space is between midday and two p.m., when local people go home for lunch.
31. Do no park in a *Zone Bleue*. Look for a public car park.
32. Try the local market for your food shopping. It is cheaper and better quality.

33. Domestic gas is usually bottled Calor gas.
34. If you have an accident, keep calm and do not lose your temper.
35. Remember that *'merci'* means 'no, thank you' until you have received the food. If you would like some, say *'je veux bien'* and then *'merci'*.
36. You are not going for three months and the weather will be warmer than in the U.K. You will not need all those clothes!
37. Do not be snobbish about wine. Try the cheap ones. You will be pleasantly surprised.
38. Secure your windows, cancel the milk and papers and tell the police when you will be away.
39. Give a relative your holiday address for emergency contact.
40. If you leave the telephone number of your hotel or campsite, relatives or friends can contact you by ringing the international operator, who will be bi-lingual.
41. It is easy to telephone home. Dial 00, 44, your dial code minus the leading zero, then the number, e.g. 00, 44, *1204, 574809
42. Yes, you *can* drink the water. If in any doubt buy bottled water.
43. Always get a receipt and check your change before you leave a shop. Later arguments will be met with a Gallic shrug!
44. Tobacconists display a red cigar-shaped sign. You can buy stamps there if the post office is closed.
45. Chemists are well qualified and willing to offer you advice about remedies for minor ailments. Pharmaceutical goods tend to be rather expensive.
46. A *Boucherie Chevaline* only sells horse meat!
47. French bread needs eating the same day. It can be revived next morning by toasting. French bread can be bought every day, even on Sundays.
48. Shopping in a supermarket avoids language problems, but it doesn't help you to practise your French!
49. If you ask for *un café* you will get a small black coffee. Ask for *café au lait* if you want a large cup of coffee with milk.

50. Have you taken account of the time difference when booking ferries and assessing arrival times?

51. Banks are sometimes closed the day before or after a bank holiday.

52. Many shops, particularly in villages, close for two hours at lunch time. Buy the food for your picnic before midday.

53. Check that your road tax and M.O.T. certificate will still be valid when you get back to Britain.

54. Expect the cost of foodstuffs to be higher than in the U.K.

55. Croissants taste even better when warmed in the oven for a few minutes before eating.

56. There are no deliveries of newspapers or milk in many parts of France.

57. If a bottle has *consigné* on it, there is money back on the bottle.

58. Milk is sold in one litre packets. Look for the word *pasteurisé*.

59. Yesterday's British newspapers will be available in some holiday resorts but are expensive.

60. When you buy French coffee, on the packet *grains* means beans and *moulu* means ground.

61. In hotels and cafés breakfast coffee may be served in bowls.

62. Shoe and clothes sizes are different from ours. See the conversion tables.

63. Dry food stuffs are sold in kilograms and liquids in litres.

64. In swimming pools you may be obliged to wear a *bonnet* (swimming cap) and a shower is usually compulsory before you swim.

65. Take lots of sweets with you for the children. They tend to be expensive.

66. Some well-known brands of chocolate bar taste different. The taste is modified to suit the French palate.

67. Some banks only allow a few customers in at a time. The door may be locked. Ring the bell for admittance.

Measures and Conversion Tables

Distance

1 mile – 1.6 kilometres
1 kilometre – 0.62 miles
1 yard – 0.91 metres
1 metre – 1.09 yards
1 foot – 0.31 metres
1 metre – 3.28 feet
1 inch – 2.54 centimetres
1 centimetre – 0.394 inches

Weight

1 lb. – 0.45 kilos
1 kilo – 2.21 lb.
½ kilo – about 1 lb.
1 oz. – 28 grams
100 grames – 3½ oz.

Capacity

1 gallon – 4.5 litres
1 litre – 0.22 gallons

Tyre Pressure

lbs./sq. inch	kg./sq. cm.
18	1.26
20	1.40
22	1.54
24	1.68
26	1.83
28	1.96
30	2.10
32	2.24

Temperature

fahrenheit	centigrade
40	4.4
50	10.0
60	15.5
70	21.1
80	26.6

centigrade	fahrenheit
10	50
20	68
30	86
40	104

98.4 F – body temp.   36.9 C

Shoes (Men's)

British	Continental
1	35
2	36
3	37
4	38
5	39
6	40
7	41
8	42
9	43
10	44
11	45
12	46
13	48

Shoes (Children's)

1	17
2	18
3	19
4	20

5	22
6	23
7	24
8	25
9	27
10	28
11	29
12	30
13	31

Shoes (Women's)

1	33
2	34
3	35
4	36
5	37
6	38
7	39
8	40

Dresses

British	Continental
34	40
36	42
38	44
40	46
42	48
44	50

Shirts and Collars

British	Continental
	36
$14\frac{1}{2}$	37
15	38
$15\frac{1}{2}$	39

16	41
16½	42
17	43

French Numbers

1 un	32 trente-deux
2 deux	33 trente-trois
3 trois	34 trente-quatre
4 quatre	35 trente-cinq
5 cinq	36 trente-six
6 six	37 trente-sept
7 sept	38 trente-huit
8 huit	39 trente-neuf
9 neuf	40 quarante
10 dix	41 quarante et un
11 onze	42 quarante-deux
12 douze	43 quarante-trois
13 treize	44 quarante-quatre
14 quatorze	45 quarante-cinq
15 quinze	46 quarante-six
16 seize	47 quarante-sept
17 dix-sept	48 quarante-huit
18 dix-huit	49 quarante-neuf
19 dix-neuf	50 cinquante
20 vingt	51 cinquante et un
21 vingt et un	52 cinquante-deux
22 vingt-deux	53 cinquante-trois
23 vingt-trois	54 cinquante-quatre
24 vingt-quatre	55 cinquante-cinq
25 vingt-cinq	56 cinquante-six
26 vingt-six	57 cinquante-sept
27 vingt-sept	58 cinquante-huit
28 vingt-huit	59 cinquante-neuf
29 vingt-neuf	60 soixante
30 trente	61 soixante et un
31 trente et un	62 soixante-deux

63 soixante-trois
64 soixante-quatre
65 soixante-cinq
66 soixante-six
67 soixante-sept
68 soixante-huit
69 soixante-neuf
70 soixante-dix
71 soixante et onze
72 soixante-douze
73 soixante-treize
74 soixante-quatorze
75 soixante-quinze
76 soixante-seize
77 soixante-dix-sept
78 soixante-dix-huit
79 soixante-dix-neuf
80 quatre-vingts
81 quatre-vingt-un
82 quatre-vingt-deux
83 quatre-vingt-trois
84 quatre-vingt-quatre
85 quatre-vingt-cinq

86 quatre-vingt-six
87 quatre-vingt-sept
88 quatre-vingt-huit
89 quatre-vingt-neuf
90 quatre-vingt-dix
91 quatre-vingt-onze
92 quatre-vingt-douze
93 quatre-vingt-treize
94 quatre-vingt-quatorze
95 quatre-vingt-quinze
96 quatre-vingt-seize
97 quatre-vingt-dix-sept
98 quatre-vingt-dix-huit
99 quatre-vingt-dix-neuf
100 cent
101 cent un
200 deux cents
257 deux cent cinquante-sept
1,000 mille
1,550 mille cinq cent cinquante
2,500 deux mille cinq cents
1,000,000 un million

How to tell the time in French

The hours

Il est une heure – **It is one o'clock.**
Il est deux heures – **It is two o'clock.**
Il est neuf heures – **It is nine o'clock.**
Il est midi – **It is (twelve o'clock) midday.**
Il est minuit – **It is (twelve o'clock) midnight.**

The minutes past the hour

First you say the hour, then you add on the minutes:

Il est une heure dix – **It is ten past one.**
Il est sept heures vingt-cinq – **It is twenty five past seven.**
Il est neuf heures vingt-deux – **It is twenty two minutes past nine.**

Quarter past

First say the hour, then add on – **et quart** or **quinze** (fifteen).

Il est trois heures et quart – **It is quarter past three.**
Il est dix heures quinze – **It is ten fifteen.**

Half past

First say the hour, then add on – **et demie** or **trente** (thirty).

Il est cinq heures et demie – **It is half past five.**
Il est deux heures trente – **It is two thirty.**

The minutes to the hour

First say the hour it is going to be, then minus the number of minutes using **moins**.

The Time at a Glance
Quelle heure est-il? – What time is it?
Il est _____ heure(s) _____

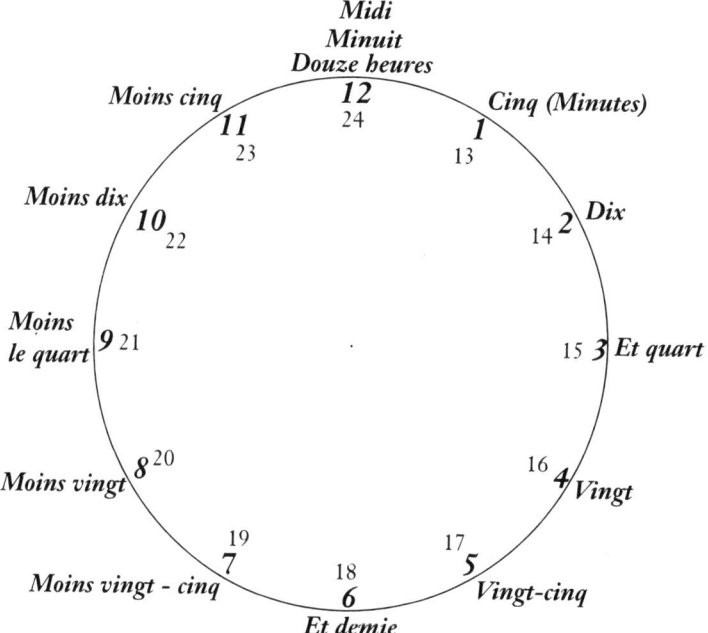

eg. It is five past one. – Il est une heure cinq.
It is quarter past eight. – Il est huit heures et quart
It is twenty to seven. – Il est sept heures moins vingt.

Il est six heures moins cinq – **It is five minutes to six**
Il est huit heures moins vingt-sept – **It is twenty seven minutes to eight**.

Quarter to

First say the hour it is going to be, then add **moins le quart**.

Il est une heure moins le quart – **It is quarter to one.**
Il est midi moins le quart – **It is quarter to twelve (midday)**.

Days of the Week

Monday – lundi
Tuesday – mardi
Wednesday – mercredi
Thursday – jeudi
Friday – vendredi
Saturday – samedi
Sunday – dimanche

Months of the year

January – janvier
February – février
March – mars
April – avril
May – mai
June – juin
July – juillet
August – août
September – septembre
October – octobre
November – novembre
December – décembre

Seasons

Spring – le printemps
Summer – l'été
Autumn – l'automne
Winter – l'hiver

Colours

Beige – beige
White – blanc, blanche
Blue – bleu, bleue
Navy blue – bleu marine
Blond – blond, blonde
Brown – brun, brune, marron
Hazel – châtain
Grey – gris, grise
Yellow – jaune
Black – noir, noire
Orange – orange
Purple – pourpre
Pink – rose
Red – rouge
Green – vert, verte
Violet – violet, violette

How to read a weather forecast

le temps – **the weather**
un bulletin météorologique – **a weather bulletin/forecast**
les prévisions météorologiques – **the weather forecast**
on prévoit – **we forecast**

Nice weather

Il fait beau, il fera beau – **it is nice, it will be nice weather.**
Il fait chaud, il fera chaud – **it is warm, it will be warm.**

Il y a (il y aura) un temps ensoleillé – **there is (will be) sunny weather.**
Il y a (il y aura) de belles éclaircies – **there are (will be) bright spells.**
Il y a (il y aura) du soleil – **there is (will be) some sun.**
Le soleil brille (va briller) – **the sun is shining (is going to shine).**
Un temps agréable (magnifique) – **pleasant (magnificent) weather.**
La chaleur – **the heat.**
Un temps sec et doux – **dry, mild weather.**

Wet weather

Il pleut, il pleuvra, il va pleuvoir – **it is raining, it will rain, it is going to rain.**
Il pleut à verse – **it is pouring with rain.**
Il est (sera) pluvieux – **it is (will be) rainy.**
Il y a (il y aura) de la pluie – **there is (will be) rain.**
Il y a (il y aura) des bruines – **there is (will be) drizzle.**
Une averse – **a shower.**
La précipitation – **rainfall.**
Un orage, une tempête – **a storm.**
Le tonnerre et les éclairs – **thunder and lightning.**
Il est (sera) humide, brumeux, orageux – **it is (will be) humid, misty, stormy.**

Wintry conditions

Il fait (fera) mauvais temps – **it is (will be) bad weather.**
Il neige, il neigera, il va neiger – **it is snowing, will snow, is going to snow.**
Il gèle, il gèlera, il va geler – **it is freezing, will freeze, is going to freeze.**
Il fait froid, il fera froid – **it is cold, it will be cold.**
Le gel, la glace, le verglas, la grêle – **frost, ice, black ice, hail.**
Il fait (fera) du brouillard – **it is (will be) foggy.**

LA METEO

SOLEIL | NUAGES | COUVERT

Mer calme

FECAMP

Mer agitée

FECAMP

LE HAVRE

Matin

LE HAVRE

BRUME | PLUIES | AVERSES | NEIGE

Après-midi

PRÉVISIONS POUR LA JOURNÉE DU SAMEDI 31 AOÛT POUR LA RÉGION DU HAVRE. — Temps : Ensoleillé avec retour de quelques petits nuages. **— Vent :** Est modéré. **— Températures prévues :** Maxi sur côte : 22 à 23° ; dans l'intérieur : 24 à 26° ; mini sur côte : 15 à 16° ; dans l'intérieur : 13 à 14°. **— Hauteur d'eau recueillie,** de 7 h le 29 à 7 h le 30 : Néant. **— Températures relevées hier au Havre :** Maxi : 27° 5 ; mini : 13° 8. **— Pression atmosphérique relevée hier :** 1.019 Hpa.

COMPLÉMENT A USAGE MARITIME. — Ciel : Ensoleillé. **— Vent :** Est à Sud-Est, 10 à 15 nœuds, force 3 à 4 le matin, venant Nord-Est, force 4 à 5 l'après-midi. **— Mer :** Peu agitée à agitée vers le large. **— Visibilité :** Supérieure à 8 milles.

TENDANCE ULTÉRIEURE. — Dimanche : temps ensoleillé et chaud.

RENSEIGNEMENTS COMPLÉMENTAIRES ENREGISTRÉS (sur répondeur téléphonique automatique). — Marine côte : 36.65.08.76. Grand public : 36.65.02.76.

METEO FRANCE

Windy weather

Il fait (fera) du vent – **it is (will be) windy.**
Un vent faible (léger) – **a slight breeze.**
Un vent frais – **a cool breeze.**
Un vent modéré, froid, fort – **a moderate, cold, strong wind.**

The sky

Le ciel est clair, bleu, gris, nuageux, couvert, lourd, triste, sombre, noir, orageux – **the sky is clear, blue, grey, cloudy, overcast, heavy, dull, gloomy, dark, stormy.**

Where?

Dans le nord, l'est, le sud, l'ouest – **in the north, east, south, west.**
Sur le nord-est de la région – **over the north-east of the region.**
Sur le sud-ouest de la France – **over the south-west of France.**
Sur la plupart des régions – **over most regions.**
Sur toute la France – **over the whole of France.**
Sur la côte – **on the coast.**
Dans le centre – **in the centre.**
A l'ombre – **in the shade.**
Des brumes fréquentes – **widespread mist.**

When?

Ce matin, cet après-midi, ce soir – **this morning, this afternoon, this evening.**
Hier, aujourd'hui, demain – **yesterday, today, tomorrow.**
En hiver, au printemps, en été, en automne – **in winter, in spring, in summer, in autumn.**
Aux premières heures de la matinée – **in the early hours of the morning.**
En début de journée – **at the beginning of the day.**
Dès la fin de la matinée – **from the end of the morning.**
Brumes matinales – **morning mists.**

En cours de l'après-midi – **during the course of the afternoon.**
En début de soir – **in the early evening.**
Au lever du soleil – **at sunrise.**
Au coucher du soleil – **at sunset.**

Other phrases

Le temps est (sera) variable – **the weather is (will be) change-able.**
Températures en baisse, en hausse – **temperatures falling, rising.**
Température maximale – **maximum temperature.**
Températures modestes pour la saison – **lowish temperatures for the season.**
Une amélioration du temps – **an improvement in the weather.**

French–English Dictionary

une abeille – bee
d'abord – firstly
un abri couvert – shed for car
un abricot – apricot
accepter – to accept
  J'accepte – I accept
  vous acceptez des chèques? – do you take cheques?
l'accès
accès direct à la plage – direct access to the beach
accès interdit – no access
un accident – accident
d'accord – agreed, okay
  Je suis d'accord – I agree
  Je ne suis pas d'accord – I do not agree
l'accueil – reception, welcome
accueillant – welcoming, hospitable
les achats – purchases
acheter – to buy
  J'achète – I buy
actif(ve) – active
les actualités – the news
l'addition – bill (café or restaurant)
  Je voudrais l'addition – I would like the bill
adorer – to adore
  J'adore – I adore
l'adresse – the address
un aéroglisseur – hovercraft
l'aéroport – airport
une affiche – placard, poster, bill

affreux – awful, terrible
une agence immobilière – estate agents
une agence de voyage – travel agents
un agent de police – policeman
un agneau – lamb
agréable – pleasant
aider – to help
  J'aide – I help
  Aidez-moi – help me
l'ail – garlic
une aile – wing
aimable – likeable, friendly, nice
aimer – to like
  J'aime – I like
aîné – elder, eldest
  J'ai un frère aîné – I have an elder brother
l'air – air
  en plein air – in the open air
l'alimentation – food
L'Allemagne – Germany
allemand – German
aller – to go
  Je vais – I go
  un aller simple – a single ticket
  un aller retour – a return ticket
allô – hello (telephone)
allumer – to light
des allumettes – matches
  une boîte d'allumettes – a box of matches

l'alpinisme – climbing, mountaineering

l'ambiance – surroundings, environment, atmosphere

une ambulance – ambulance

une amélioration – improvement

améliorer – to improve

aménagé – fitted (bedroom or kitchen)

une amende – fine (legal)

un(e) ami(e) – friend

amical – friendly

l'amitié – friendship

amitiés à tous – best wishes to everyone

s'amuser – to enjoy oneself

  Je m'amuse – I am enjoying myself

  Amusez-vous bien! – Have a good time!

amusant – funny

un an – year

un ananas – pineapple

une année – year

  Ouvert toute l'année – open all the year round

ancien – old

une andouille – chitterling

un âne – donkey

anglais – English

Je suis anglais – I am English

l'Angleterre – England

un animal domestique – pet

un anniversaire – birthday, anniversary

une annonce – notice, advertisement

un annuaire – telephone directory

un apéritif – aperitif, appetizer, drink (before meal)

un appareil (photo) – camera

un appartement – flat

s'appeler – to be called

  Je m'appelle – I am called

appétissant – appetizing, tempting

l'appétit – appetite

  bon appétit – have a nice meal

apporter – to bring

  apportez-moi – bring me

apprécier – to appreciate

  J'apprécie – I appreciate

approuver – to approve

  J'approuve – I approve

appuyez (sur le bouton) – press (the button)

après – after

l'après-midi – the afternoon

une araignée – spider

un arbre – tree

l'argent – money

l'argent de poche – pocket money

  Je n'ai pas d'argent – I have no money

une armoire – wardrobe

un arrêt d'autobus – bus stop

s'arrêter – to stop

  Arrêtez! – Stop!

les arrhes – deposit (money)

l'arrière – behind, back

arriver – to arrive

  J'arrive – I arrive

un artichaut – artichoke

un ascenseur – lift

un aspirateur – vacuum cleaner

  Je passe l'aspirateur – I do the hoovering

une aspirine – aspirin

assez – enough, quite

  J'en ai assez! – I've had enough!

  assez bien – quite good

une assiette – plate

assiette anglaise – starter consisting of cold meats

asseyez-vous – sit down

assis – sitting, seated

l'asperge – asparagus

un atelier – studio, workshop

attendre – to wait

   J'attends – I wait

   Attendez! – Wait!

attention! – careful! watch out!

une auberge – inn, small hotel

une auberge de jeunesse – youth hostel

aujourd'hui – today

au revoir – goodbye

aussi – also

une auto – car

un autobus – bus

un autocar – coach

l'automne – autumn

   en automne – in autumn

une autoroute – motorway

l'autostop – hitch-hiking

avaler – to swallow

   Je ne peux pas avaler – I can't swallow

avant – before

avec – with

   et avec ça? – anything else? (in a shop)

une averse – (sudden) shower, downpour

un avion – aeroplane

l'aviron – rowing

l'avis – opinion

   à mon avis – in my opinion

un avocat – lawyer

avoir – to have

   J'ai – I have

   Avez-vous? – Have you got?

avril – April

baba au rhum – rum baba (cake)

les bagages – luggage

une bague – ring (jewellery)

une baguette – French stick (bread)

la baignade – bathing

   baignade interdite – no bathing

se baigner – to bathe

   Je me baigne – I go bathing

une baignoire – bath (tub)

un bain – bath

   prendre un bain – to have a bath

un bal – dance

un bal travesti – fancy dress dance

un balcon – balcony, dress-circle (theatre)

un ballon – (large) ball

un banc – bench

une banque – bank (money)

une barbe à papa – candy floss

un bas – stocking

en bas – downstairs

un bateau – boat

un bâtiment – building

une batterie – battery

beau (belle) – beautiful, attractive

   il fait beau – it is nice weather

beaucoup – a lot, many

   merci beaucoup – thank you very much

un bébé – baby

beige – beige (colour)

un beignet – a fritter

belle (*see* **beau**)

bête – stupid

une betterave – beetroot

le beurre – butter

une bibliothèque – library

une bicyclette – a bicycle

la bière – beer
   à la pression – draught
   en bouteille – bottled
bière brune – dark beer
bière blonde – light beer
bien – well, good
un bifteck – steak
une bijouterie – jeweller's shop
un billet – ticket
   un carnet de billets – a book of tickets
   un billet de banque – bank note
   un billet de 100 francs – a 100 franc note
un bistro – pub, small restaurant
blanc (blanche) – white
blessé – injured
bleu – blue
un bloc sanitaire – washrooms
blond – blond
le boeuf – beef
boire – to drink
   Je bois – I drink
   Qu'est-que vous voulez boire? – What do you want to drink?
un bois – wood (forest)
une boisson – drink
   boissons pilote – drinks list
une boîte – box, tin
une boîte aux lettres – letter box
une boîte d'allumettes – a box of matches
un bol – bowl
bon (bonne) – good
bon appétit – have a nice meal
bon marché – cheap
bonne chance – good luck
des bonbons – sweets
bonjour – hello, good day

des bottes – boots
la bouche – mouth
le boucher — the butcher
une boucherie – butcher's shop
une boucherie chevaline – a horse meat butcher's
une boucle d'oreille – earring
bouclé – buckled, fastened
   les cheveux bouclés – curly hair
une bougie – candle, spark plug (car)
bouillant – boiling
le boulanger – baker
une boulangerie – baker's
boules – bowls (game)
au bout de – at the end of
une bouteille – bottle
une boutique – small shop
un bracelet – bracelet
le bras – arm
une brasserie – pub, restaurant
la Bretagne – Brittany
La Grande Bretagne – Great Britain
le bricolage – D.I.Y.
un briquet – lighter
britannique – British
une brochure — brochure, leaflet
bronzé – suntanned
se bronzer – to get a tan
   Je suis bronzé – I've got a tan
une brosse à cheveux – hairbrush
une brosse à dents – toothbrush
se brosser – to brush
   Je me brosse les dents – I brush my teeth
le brouillard – fog
   Il fait du brouillard – it is foggy
la bruine – drizzle
un bruit – noise

la brume – mist
brumeux – misty
brun – brown
bruyant – noisy
un buffet – refreshment bar
un bulletin – report
un bureau – office
bureau d'accueil – reception office
bureau de change – money exchange office

une cabine téléphonique – telephone booth
un cabinet de médecin – doctor's surgery
une cacahuète – peanut
un cachet (d'aspirine) – tablet (aspirin)
un cadeau – present, gift
cadet(te) – younger, youngest
un café – a café
le café – coffee
   au lait – with milk
   crème – with cream
   café moulu – ground coffee
   café à grains – coffee beans
une cafetière – coffee pot
un cahier – exercise book
une caisse – till, cash desk, checkout
Caisse d'Epargne – name of a bank
une calculatrice – calculator
calme – calm
un camion – lorry
une camionnette – van
la campagne – countryside
   à la campagne – in the country
un camping – a camp site

faire le camping – to go camping
un canapé – couch, settee
un canapé-lit – bed settee
un canard – duck
un canif – penknife
une carafe – jug, carafe
une caravane – caravan
un carnet (de billets) – book (of tickets)
un carnet de chèques – a cheque book
une carotte – carrot
carré – square (in shape)
à carreaux – check (pattern)
une carte – map, menu, card
une carte d'adhérent – membership card
une carte d'anniversaire – birthday card
une carte d'identité – identity card
une carte postale – postcard
une carte des vins – winelist
se casser – to break
   Je me suis cassé le bras – I've broken my arm
un casse-croûte – snack
une casserole – pan
une cathédrale – cathedral
une caution – deposit (money)
Ça va? – are you well?
Ça va bien – I am very well
une cave – a (wine) cellar
Cédez le passage – Give Way (road sign)
une ceinture – belt
une ceinture en cuir – leather belt
une ceinture de sécurité – seat belt
célèbre – famous

célibataire – single (unmarried)
un cellier – cellar
une centaine – about 100
un centime – one hundredth of a
   franc
un centimètre – centimetre
un centre commercial – shopping
   centre
le centre-ville – town centre
les céréales – cereals
une cerise – cherry
une chaise – chair
la chaleur – heat
une chambre – bedroom
Chambre d'Hôte – bed and
   breakfast hotel
des champignons – mushrooms
un chandail – sweater
changer – to change
   Je change – I change
   il faut changer? – do I have to
      change? (trains)
un chapeau – hat
la charcuterie – cooked meats
   (shop)
un chariot – a supermarket trolley
charmant – charming
la chasse – hunting
un chat – cat
un château – castle, country man-
   sion
chaud – warm, hot
   il fait chaud – it is hot (weather)
   J'ai chaud – I am hot
le chauffage – heating
le chauffage par convecteurs –
   convector heating
le chauffage à accumulation –
   storage heating
le chauffage au mazout – oil fired
   heating

chauffé – heated
un chauffeur – driver
chaussée déformée – uneven road
   surface (road sign)
des chaussettes – socks
des chaussures — shoes
un chemin – path, way, road
le chemin de fer – railway
un chemin privé – private road
une cheminée – fireplace
une chemise – shirt
un chèque (de voyage) – (traveller's) cheque
cher – dear, expensive
   c'est trop cher – it's too dear
chercher – to look for
   Je cherche – I'm looking for
   va chercher – go and find, go
      and get
un cheval — horse
les cheveux – hair
une cheville – ankle
une chèvre – goat
le chewing gum – chewing gum
chic – smart, stylish
un chien – dog
chien méchant! – beware of the
   dog!
des chips – (potato) crisps
choisir – to choose
   Je choisis – I choose
le choix – choice
   au choix – a choice of
un chou – cabbage
un chou-fleur – cauliflower
des choux de Bruxelles – Brussels
   sprouts
chut! – hush! Ssh!
le cidre – cider
un cinéma – cinema
la circulation – traffic

un citron – lemon
citron pressé – lemon squash
clair – clear, bright
un classeur écolier – a school file
une clé/clef – key
un client – customer
clignoter – to signal
un clignotant – car direction indicator
clos – closed in, enclosed
un cochon – pig
une cocotte – stew pan
une cocotte-minute – pressure cooker
le coeur – heart
  J'ai mal au coeur – I feel sick
un coffre – car boot
un coffre-fort – safe, strong box
un coiffeur (une coiffeuse) – hairdresser
un coin – corner
  coin cuisine – corner kitchen
  au coin de la rue – at the street corner
un collant – ladies' tights
un collier – a necklace
combien – how much, how many
  c'est combien? – how much is it?
les comestibles – provisions, food
commander – to order
  Je peux commander? – Can I order?
commencer – to begin
  Je commence – I begin
un commerçant – shopkeeper
un commerce – shop, business
le commissariat – police station
les commissions – the shopping
  faire les commissions – to do the shopping

complet – full
compliqué – complicated
composez (le numéro) – dial (the number)
des comprimés – tablets
compris – included, understood
  service compris – service charge included
un comptoir – counter (shop)
un concombre – cucumber
une confiserie – sweet shop
la confiture – jam
confiture d'oranges – marmalade
confortable – comfortable
le congé (annuel) – (annual) leave
  un jour de congé – a day off
un congélateur – freezer
la consigne – left luggage office
consigné – there is money back on the bottle
constipé – constipated
content – happy
continuer – to continue
  Je continue – I continue
une contravention – parking ticket
un copain (une copine) – friend, pal, mate
les coquillages – shell fish
la cordonnerie – shoe maker's
un cornichon – gherkin
un costume – dress, suit
la côte – coast
à côté (de) – at the side (of)
  côté de stationnement – parking side
en coton – made of cotton
coton hydrophile – cottonwool
le cou – neck
le coucher du soleil – sunset
se coucher – to go to bed

Je me couche – I go to bed
une couchette – cot, berth, bunk
le coude – elbow
la couleur – colour
une coupure – cut (injury)
une cour – yard
une cour close – an enclosed yard
une courgette – courgette, marrow
courir – to run
  Je cours – I run
le courrier – mail, post
une courroie de ventilateur – fanbelt (car)
le cours de change – the exchange rate
une course – race
les courses – the shopping
  faire les courses – to do the shopping
court – short
un(e) cousin(e) – cousin
un couteau – knife
coûter – to cost
  Ça coûte combien? – How much does that cost?
couvert – covered
  piscine couverte – indoor swimming pool
  couvert compris – cover charge included (restaurant)
une couverture – a blanket
une cravate – tie
un crayon – pencil
Crédit Agricole – name of bank
Crédit Mutuelle – name of bank
la crème – cream
une crémerie – dairy (shop)
une crêpe – pancake
une crêperie – pancake shop/stall

un croissant – croissant, crescent shaped bread roll
un croque-monsieur – toasted cheese sandwich
un croque-madame – toasted cheese sandwich with egg on top
une cuillère – spoon
le cuir – leather
  en cuir – made of leather
la cuisine – kitchen
  faire la cuisine – to do the cooking
une cuisinière – cooker, cook
cuit – cooked
  bien cuit – well cooked (steak)
un cyclomoteur – moped

une dame – a lady
dames – ladies' toilet
dangereux – dangerous
danser – to dance
  Je danse – I dance
la date – the date
débarrasser la table – to clear the table
décembre – december
décrochez le combiné – lift the receiver (telephone)
déçu – disappointed
défendu (de) – it is prohibited
défense de – do not
dégoûtant – disgusting
la dégustation – tasting
dehors – outside
le déjeuner – lunch
un delco – distributor (car)
délicieux – delicious
demander – to ask
  Je demande – I ask
démarrer – to start (car)

ma voiture ne démarre pas – my car won't start

demi – half

demi-douzaine – half a dozen

demi-heure – half an hour

demi-litre – half a litre

demi-sec – medium dry (wine)

demi-tarif – half price

les dents – teeth

J'ai mal aux dents – I have toothache

le dentifrice – toothpaste

le dentiste – dentist

dépanner – to repair or fix

une dépanneuse – break-down lorry

dépasser – to overtake

des dépendances – outbuildings

dépenser – to spend (money)

un dépliant – leaflet, brochure

déranger – to disturb

Je vous dérange? – Am I disturbing you?

dernier – last, latest

derrière – behind

désagréable – unpleasant

descendre – to go down, get off (vehicle)

Je descends – I get off

descendez ici – get off here

se déshabiller — to get undressed

Je me déshabille – I get undressed

au-dessus – above

au-dessous – below

détester – to hate

Je déteste – I hate

deux – two

deuxième – second

devant – in front of

devenir – to become

Je deviens – I become

une déviation – diversion (road)

devoir – to have to

Je dois – I must

les devoirs – homework

Je fais mes devoirs – I do my homework

la diarrhée – diarrhoea

J'ai la diarrhée – I've got the runs

Dieu – God

Mon Dieu! – My God!

difficile – difficult

un digestif – drink taken after meals to aid digestion

dimanche – Sunday

une dinde – turkey

le dîner – evening meal

direct – direct

C'est direct? – Is it direct? (train)

la direction – direction

toutes directions – all directions (for through traffic)

une discothèque – disco

disponible – available

un disque – record

des distractions – entertainments, amenities

un divan – settec, couch

divorcé – divorced

un doigt – finger

le domicile habituel – usual address

donner – to give

Je donne – I give

donnez-moi – give me

dormir – to sleep

Je dors – I sleep

Je ne peux pas dormir – I can't sleep

un **dortoir** – dormitory
le **dos** – back (body)
la **douane** – customs (post)
une **douche** – shower
la **douleur** – pain
doux – sweet, soft, smooth
une **douzaine** – dozen
un **drap** – sheet, cloth
un **drapeau** – flag
une **droguerie** – hardware shop
dur – hard
durer – to last
    ça dure combien de temps? –
    how long does it last?
un **duvet** – sleeping bag, duvet

l'**eau** – water
l'**eau chaude** – hot water
l'**eau froide** – cold water
l'**eau minérale** – mineral water
l'**eau (non) potable** – (not) drink-
    ing water
l'**eau-de-vie** – brandy, spirit
un **échange** – exchange
    faire un échange – to go on an
    exchange
échanger – to exchange
une **éclaircie** – bright, sunny spell
éclairé – lit up
une **école** – school
des **économies** – savings
    faire des économies – to save up
l'**Ecosse** – Scotland
écossais – scottish
écouter – to listen
    J'écoute – I am listening
    Ecoutez! – Listen!
écrire – to write
    J'écris – I write
    écris-moi bientôt – write to me
    soon

égal – equal
    ça m'est égal – it's all the same
    to me
une **église** – church
un **électrophone** – record player
l'**emballage** – packaging
un **embouteillage** – traffic jam
l'**embrayage** – clutch (car)
une **émission** – programme
un **emplacement** – place, pitch
    (on a campsite)
à **emporter** – take away (food)
emprunter – to borrow
    Je peux emprunter? – Can I
    borrow?
un **endroit** – place, spot, location
énervé – irritable, nervy
un **enfant** – child
enfin – at last, finally
ennuyeux – boring
énorme – enormous
enrhumé (Je suis) – (I am) full of
    a cold
ensoleillé – sunny
ensuite – then, next
entendre – to hear
    J'entends – I hear
entre – between
une **entrée** – entrance, first course
    (meal)
    entrée libre – free entry (in a
    walk round store)
entrer – to enter
    J'entre – I enter
    entrez – come in
une **enveloppe** – envelope
environ – about, approximately
    dans les environs – in the vi-
    cinity
envoyer – to send
    Je t'envoie – I am sending you

Je voudrais envoyer – I would like to send
l'épaule – shoulder
une épicerie – grocer's shop
l'épicier – grocer
éplucher – to peel
un éplucheur – a peeler
épouvantable – terrible, awful
épuisé – exhausted
une équipe – team
l'équitation – horse riding
une erreur – a mistake
  Je pense qu'il y a une erreur – I think there has been a mistake
un escalier – staircase
un escalier roulant – an escalator
espérer – to hope
  J'espère – I hope
essayer – to try, try on (clothes)
  Je peux l'essayer? – Can I try it on?
  un salon d'essayage – a changing room (clothes shop)
l'essence – petrol
les essuie-glaces – windscreen wipers
essuyer – to wipe
  J'essuie – I wipe
  Je m'essuie – I wipe myself
l'Est – the East
un étage – floor, storey
  à l'étage – on the upper floor
  au premier étage – on the first floor
une étagère – shelf
l'état – state, condition
  en bon/mauvais état – in good/bad condition
l'été – summer
  en été – in summer

une étiquette – label
une étoile – star
étrange – strange, foreign
un étranger – stranger, foreigner
étroit – narrow
un(e) étudiant(e) – student
étudier – to study
  J'étudie – I study
un évier – sink (kitchen)
une excursion – a trip out
  faire une excursion – to go on a trip
excusez-moi – excuse me
à l'extérieur – outside

en face de – facing, opposite
facile – easy
faible – weak
le faim – hunger
  J'ai faim – I am hungry
  avez-vous faim? – are you hungry?
faire – to do, make
  Je fais – I do
faites le plein – fill the tank (petrol)
une famille – family
fatigué – tired
il faut – it is necessary
un fauteuil – armchair
un fauteuil-lit – bed settee
faux – false
félicitations! – congratulations!
une femme – woman, wife
femmes – ladies' toilet
une fenêtre – window
un fer (à repasser) – electric iron
fériés, jours fériés (bank) holidays
fermé – closed
fermer – to close
  Je ferme – I close

fermez la porte – close the door

la fermeture annuelle (hebdomadairè) – annual (weekly) closing days

une fermeture éclair – zip fastener

un ferry – ferry

une fête – festival, holiday, celebration, festivity

un feu – fire
   Au feu! – Fire!

un feu de camp – camp fire

des feux d'artifice – fireworks

des feux rouges – traffic lights

février – February

une ficelle – slim french stick (bread)

une fiche de voyageur – (hotel) registration card

une fièvre – a temperature
   J'ai la fièvre – I have a temperature

une fille – girl, daughter
   une petite-fille – granddaughter

un fils – son
   un petit-fils – grandson

la fin – end

finir – to finish
   Je finis – I finish

un flacon – small bottle (perfume, washing up liquid)

une fleur – flower

le foie – liver

foncé – dark (coloured)

fonctionner – to work, function
   ça ne fonctionne pas – it's not working

une forêt – forest

formidable – great, tremendous

un formulaire – form (to fill in)

fou – mad, stupid

un four – oven

une fourchette – fork

frais (fraîche) – fresh (food), cool (wind)

une fraise – strawberry
   une glace à la fraise – strawberry ice cream

une framboise – raspberry

un franc – franc (money)

français – French

la France – France

frappé – chilled, iced
   whisky frappé – whisky on the rocks

frapper – to knock
   Je frappe – I knock
   frappez – knock

freiner – to brake (car)

les freins – brakes (car)

un frère – brother

un frigo – fridge

frit – fried

des frites – chips

une friture – fry (esp. fried fish)

froid – cold
   il fait froid – it is cold
   J'ai froid – I am cold

le fromage – cheese

le fruit – fruit

fruits de mer – sea food

gagner – to win, earn
   Je gagne – I win, earn
   J'ai gagné! – I've won!

Galeries Lafayette – well known department store

une galette – type of cake, biscuit

Galles, Pays de Galles – Wales

gallois – Welsh

un garage – garage
un garçon – boy, waiter
un gardien – warden, caretaker, guardian
une gare SNCF – railway station
gare routière – bus station
garni – garnished (often with vegetables)
le gas-oil – diesel oil
un gâteau – cake
à gauche – on the left
gazeux(se) – fizzy (drinks)
un gendarme – policeman
la gendarmerie – police station
généralement – usually, normally
le genou – knee
gentil – kind, nice
un gérant – manager, director
un gîte – country house, cottage
une glace – ice cream, mirror
glacé – frozen, chilled
un glacier – ice cream man
un glaçon – ice cube
gonflé – puffy, swollen
la gorge – throat
  J'ai mal à la gorge – I have a sore throat
le goût – taste
goûter – to taste
le graissage – greasing, lubrication
une gramme – gram (weight)
grand – big, tall
gras – fatty
gratuit – free of charge
grave – serious
gravement (blessé) – seriously (injured)
un grenier – loft, attic
une grenouille – frog
une grève – strike (industrial)
grillé – grilled

la grippe – flu
  J'ai la grippe – I have the flu
gris – grey
gros (grosse) – stout, fat
des groseilles – redcurrants
une guêpe – wasp
un guichet – ticket office, turnstile, pay desk

s'habiller – to get dressed
  Je m'habille – I get dressed
habiter – to live
  J'habite – I live
  où habitez-vous? – where do you live?
d'habitude – usually
la hanche – hip
des haricots verts – green beans
en haut – up there, upstairs
hebdomadaire – weekly
l'hébergement – accommodation
hein? – Eh? what?
l'herbe – grass
l'heure – time
  à l'heure – on time
  à tout à l'heure – see you later
  quelle heure est-il? – what time is it?
heures d'ouverture – opening hours
heureux – happy
heurter – to crash into
hier – yesterday
l'hiver – winter
  en hiver – in winter
un homme – a man
hommes – men's toilet
honnête – honest, honourable
un hôpital – hospital
un horaire – time table

une horloge – clock (town or church)
des hors d'oeuvres – starter (meal)
hors de saison – out of season
hors de service – not working
un hôtel – hotel
un hôtel de ville – town hall
un hovercraft – hovercraft (see also aéroglisseur)
l'huile – oil
huile d'olive – olive oil
huile de tournesol – surflower oil
l'humeur – humour, mood
    de bonne (mauvaise) humeur – in a good (bad) mood
l'hypermarché – very large supermarket

ici – here
    près d'ici – near here
une idée – idea
    bonne idée! – good idea!
une île – island
il y a – there is, there are
une image – picture
un immeuble – block of flats
un imperméable – raincoat, waterproof
important – important, serious (incident)
n'importe où – anywhere
n'importe quand – anytime
n'importe qui – anyone
n'importe quoi – anything
imprévu – unforeseen
inattendu – unexpected
un incendie – (outbreak of) fire
    échelle à incendie – fire escape
incliné – sloping
inclus – enclosed

inquiet — worried, anxious
    Je suis inquiet au sujet de mon frère – I am worried about my brother
des installations – fittings, facilities
insupportable – intolerable
interdiction – prohibition, forbidding
interdit – forbidden, not allowed
intéressant – interesting
s'intéresser à – to be interested in
    Je m'intéresse à – I am intersted in
à l'intérieur – inside
irlandais – Irish
l'Irlande (du Nord) – (Northern) Ireland

jamais – never
une jambe – leg
le jambon – ham
janvier – January
un jardin – garden
jardin clos – enclosed garden
un jardin public – park
un jardin zoologique – zoo
jaune – yellow
un jean – pair of jeans
un jeu – game
jeudi – Thursday
jeune – young
joli – pretty
jouer – to play
    Je joue – I play
un jouet – toy
un joueur – player
un journal – newspaper
journalier – daily
une journée – day (time)

pendant la journée – during the day time

toute la journée – all day long

bonne journée – have a good day

juillet – July

juin – June

une jupe – skirt

un jus de fruit – fruit juice

jusqu'à – until, as far as

juste – right, correct

c'est juste – that's right

un kilo(gramme) – kilogram (weight)

un kilomètre – kilometre (distance)

là – there

là-bas – over there

un lac – lake

laid – ugly

la laine – wool

en laine – made of wool

pur laine – pure wool

le lait – milk

une laitue – lettuce

une lampe électrique – electric lamp, torch

une langue – tongue (mouth), language

langue étrangère – foreign language

un lapin – rabbit

large – wide

un lavabo – washbasin

le lavage – washing (of pots, linen, cars)

se laver – to have a wash

Je me lave – I have a wash

un lave-vaisselle – dishwasher

une laverie – washhouse, laundry

laverie automatique – launderette

le lèche-vitrines – window shopping

Je fais du lèche-vitrines – I go window shopping

un lecteur laser – a C.D. player

la lecture – reading

léger – light (weight)

un légume – vegetable

la lessive – detergent, washing

Je fais la lessive – I do the washing

un flacon de lessive liquide – a bottle of washing liquid

une lettre – letter

il y a une lettre pour moi? – is there a letter for me?

la levée – (post) collection

le lever du soleil – sunrise

se lever – to get up

Je me lève – I get up

levez-vous – get up, stand up

une librairie – bookshop

libre – free, vacant

libre-service – self service

un lièvre – hare

la limonade – lemonade

le linge – linen (sheets, towels)

lire – to read

Je lis – I read

une liste – list

un lit – bed

lit de camp – camp bed

lit d'enfant – cot

grand lit – double bed

lit à une personne – single bed

un litre – litre (liquid measure)

la livraison – delivery

un livre – book

une livre – pound (sterling), pound (weight)
la location – hire
location de vélos – bike hire
un logement – accommodation
loin – far
  c'est loin? – is it far?
  ce n'est pas loin – it's not far
les loisirs – leisure (activities)
long – long
longtemps – for a long time
à louer – for hire
lourd – heavy
  poids lourds – heavy lorry
le loyer – rent
une lumière – light
lumière du soleil – sunlight
lundi – Monday
des lunettes – glasses
lunettes de soleil – sunglasses

une machine à laver – washing machine
un magasin – shop
  un grand magasin – a department store
un magazine – a magazine
un magnétophone – tape recorder
un magnétoscope – video recorder
mai – May
un maillot – shirt, T-shirt
un maillot de bain – swimming costume
la main – hand
la mairie – town hall (small)
une maison – house
maison des jeunes – youth club
maison indépendante – detached house

mal – badly, ill
  pas mal – not bad
  avoir mal – to be ill, to hurt
  J'ai mal – I am hurting
  ça fait mal – it hurts
malade – ill
  Je me sens malade – I feel ill
une maladie – illness
un malaise – discomfort
malheureusement – unfortunately
malheureux – unhappy, unfortunate
la Manche – English channel
un mandat – money order
un manège – roundabout (fairground)
manger – to eat
  Je mange – I eat
manquer – to miss
  J'ai manqué le train – I have missed the train
un manteau – coat
le maquillage – make up
le marc – strong local brandy
un marchand – shopkeeper
marchand de vins – wine merchant
marchand de journaux — newsagent
un marché – market
marché aux puces – flea market
marcher – to walk, work
  ça ne marche pas – it doesn't work
mardi – Tuesday
la marée (basse, haute) – tide (low, high)
un mari – husband
marié – married
une marque – make, brand

marrant – funny

marre. J'en ai marre – I am fed up

marron – brown

mars – March

un matelas pneumatique – lilo, airbed

la matière grasse – fatty food

le matin – morning

matinal – morning

brume matinale – morning mist

la matinée – morning

mauvais – bad

    il fait mauvais temps – it is bad weather

un mécanicien – mechanic

méchant – naughty

    chien méchant – beware of the dog

un médicament – medicine

un médecin – doctor

le meilleur – best

le ménage – housework

    faire le ménage – to do the housework

la mer – sea

    au bord de la mer – at the seaside

    mal de mer – seasickness

mercredi – Wednesday

merveilleux – marvellous

une messe – (Catholic) mass

messieurs – gentlemen

la météo – weather forecast

un métier – job, trade

un mètre – metre (measure)

mettre – to put (on)

    Je mets – I put (on)

    Se mettre en route – to set off

meublé – furnished

des meubles – furniture

Michelin Rouge – well known hotel guide

midi – midday

le miel – honey

mieux – better

    ça va mieux? – are you better?

mignon – sweet, cute

mille – thousand

mince – thin, slim

minuit – midnight

une minute – minute

    attendez une minute – wait a minute

moche – rotten, lousy, poor, shoddy

moins – less, minus

un mois – month

une moitié – half

à moitié prix – at half price

le monde – the world

    tout le monde – everybody

    beaucoup de monde – a lot of people

Monoprix – name of a popular supermarket

monter – to climb, get on (vehicle)

    Je monte – I climb, get on

    monter une tente – to put up a tent

une montre – wrist watch

une moquette – fitted carpet

un morceau – piece

une morsure – a bite

le moteur – engine

une moto – motorcycle

un mouchoir – handkerchief

moyen – average, middle

    de taille moyenne – of average size

un moulin à café – coffee mill, grinder

un mouton – sheep, mutton
un mur – wall
mûr – ripe, mature
un musée – museum

nager – to swim
  Je nage – I swim
la naissance – birth
  date de naissance – date of birth
  lieu de naissance – place of birth
une nappe – tablecloth
la natation – swimming
nautique – relating to water
  ski nautique – water skiing
  sports nautiques – water sports
né – born
  Je suis né – I was born
nécessaire – necessary
neiger – to snow
  il neige – it is snowing
le nettoyage à sec – dry cleaning
nettoyer – to clean
  Je nettoie – I clean
neuf – nine
neuf, neuve – brand new
un neveu – nephew
le nez – nose
une nièce – niece
le niveau – level
niveau de l'eau – water level
Noël – Christmas
un noeud – knot
noir – black
une noix de coco – coconut
un nom – name
nom de famille – surname
nombreux – numerous
le Nord – North
normalement – normally, usually

la note – (hotel) bill
un nounours – teddy bear
la nourriture – food
nous – we, us
nouveau, nouvelle – new
les nouvelles – the news
Nouvelles Galeries – well known department store
novembre – November
un nuage – cloud
nuageux – cloudy
la nuit – night
  par nuit – per night
  une nuitée – one night's accommodation
nul – hopeless
  Je suis nul en Français – I am hopeless at French
un numéro de téléphone – telephone number
  un faux numéro – wrong number
en nylon – made of nylon

objets trouvés (bureau des) – lost property office
occasion – second hand
une occasion – opportunity
occupé – engaged (toilet)
s'occuper de – to attend to, to be busy with something
  Je m'occupe des enfants – I am seeing to the children
octobre – October
une odeur – odour, smell
un oeil – eye
un oeuf – egg
l'office de tourisme – tourist office
offrir — to offer
  J'offre – I offer

c'est pour offrir – it is for a present (shop)
une oie – goose
un oignon – onion
un oiseau – bird
l'ombre – shade
  à l'ombre – in the shade
une ombrelle – sunshade, parasol
un oncle – uncle
onze – eleven
l'opératrice – operator
un opticien – optician
l'or – gold
  en or – made of gold
un orage – storm
une orange – orange
l'orangina – fizzy orange drink
à l'orchestre – in the stalls (theatre)
l'ordinaire – 2 star petrol
un ordinateur – computer
une ordonnance – prescription
les ordures – rubbish
l'oreille – ear
un oreiller – pillow
ou – or
où – where
oublier – to forget
  J'ai oublié – I have forgotten
l'ouest – West
un outil – tool, utensil
ouvert – open
ouverture (heures d') – hours of opening
un ouvre-boîte – tin opener
un ouvre-bouteille – bottle-opener
ouvrir – to open
  J'ouvre – I open

le pain – bread

pain complet – wholemeal bread
  petit pain – bread roll
pain grillé – toast
une paire (de) – a pair (of)
pâle – pale
le palier – landing
une pamplemousse – grapefruit
un panier – basket
une panne – failure, breakdown
panne d'électricité – power-cut
panne d'essence – out of petrol
  Je suis tombé en panne – I've broken down
un panneau – sign, notice
un pansement – dressing, bandage
un pantalon – pants, trousers
des pantoufles – slippers
une papeterie – stationer's shop
le papier – paper
les papiers – papers, form of identity
un papillon – butterfly
Pâques – Easter
un paquet – parcel, packet
un parapluie – umbrella
un parasol – parasol, sunshade
un parc – park
un pare-brise – windscreen
un parent – parent
paresseux (euse) – lazy
parfait – perfect
parfois – sometimes
le parfum – perfume
une parfumerie – perfume shop
un parking – car park
parler – to talk, speak
  Je parle – I speak
à part – apart from
partager – to share
  Je partage – I share
partir – to leave

Je pars – I leave
à partir de – as from
à partir de lundi – from Monday
onwards
participer – to participate
  Je participe – I take part in
particulier – private
  une maison particulière – a
  private house
partout – everywhere
pas mal – not bad
pas tellement – not very much
passage protégé – you have right
of way (road sign)
passer – to pass
  Je passe – I pass, spend (time)
un passetemps – pastime, hobby
passionnant – exciting, fascinating
une pastille – a lozenge
le pâté – pâté
les pâtes – pasta
le patinage – skating
patinage à glace – ice skating
patinage à roulettes – roller-
skating
patiner – to skate
  Je patine – I skate
une patinoire – skating rink
une pâtisserie – cake shop
le patron – boss, owner
pauvre – poor
payant – paying
  parking payant – a carpark
  where you have to pay
payer – to pay
  Je paie – I pay
  Je voudrais payer – I would like
  to pay
un pays – country
le paysage – scenery, landscape
un paysan – peasant

P.C.V. – reverse charges
  **Je voudrais téléphoner en
  P.C.V.** – I would like to reverse the charges
péage – toll booth (motorway)
la peau – skin
une pêche – peach
pêcher – to fish
  Je pêche – I fish
un peigne – comb
une peinture – painting
une pellicule – film (camera)
la pelote – ball game (in S.W.
France)
une pelouse – lawn
penché – leaning
une pendule – clock
pénible – tiresome, tedious
une pension – hotel, boarding
house
  demi-pension – half board
pension complète – full board
un perce-boîtes – tin opener
perdre – to lose
  J'ai perdu – I have lost
Périphérique – ring road round
Paris
un permis (de conduire) – (driving) licence
le persil – parsley
peser – to weigh
  Je pèse – I weigh
la pétanque – French bowls
pétillant – sparkling (wine)
le petit déjeuner – breakfast
un petit-fils – grandson
une petite-fille – granddaughter
des petits gris – type of snails
des petits pois – peas
peu – little

J'ai peu d'argent – I have little money

un peu – a little

la peur – fear

J'ai peur – I am frightened

peut-être – perhaps

un phare – lighthouse, headlight (car)

une pharmacie – chemist's

une phrase – phrase, sentence

une pièce – coin, room, theatre play

la pièce – each (fruit etc.)

une pièce d'identité – identification (passport etc.)

un pied – foot

à pied – on foot

un piéton – pedestrian

une voie piétonne – pedestrian precinct

une pile – battery (torch)

une pilule – pill

pis – worse

tant pis! – too bad! hard luck!

un piquet – tent peg

un pique-nique – picnic

pîquer – to sting

une pîqure – injection

une piscine – swimming pool

une pistache – pistachio nut

une piste – slope (ski)

une piste cyclable – cycle lane

pittoresque – picturesque

un placard – cupboard

une place – place, seat

sur place – on the spot

le plafond – ceiling

une plage – beach

une plaie – wound, injury

plaire – to please

s'il vous plaît – please

se plaindre – to complain

Je veux me plaindre – I wish to complain

un plan – a plan

un plan de la ville – street plan

un plan d'eau – stretch of water

la planche à voile – windsurfing

le plancher – floor

une plaque d'immatriculation – car number plate

en plastique – made of plastic

plat – flat

un plat – dish

plat cuisiné – cooked dish

plat du jour – dish of the day

un plateau – tray

le plâtre – plaster

plâtre de moulage – plaster of Paris

il pleut – it is raining

pleuvoir – to rain

la plongée sous marine – sub-aqua diving

de plus en plus – more and more

plusieurs – several

pluvieux – rainy

un pneu – tyre

pneu crevé – punctured tyre

une poche – pocket

une poêle – frying pan

un poêle – stove

poêle à charbon – coal stove

le poids – weight

poids lourd – heavy lorry

le poignet – wrist

à point – medium (steak)

poli – polite

la pointure – (shoe) size

une poire – pear

un poireau – leek

des pois mangetout – peas (pod can be eaten)

des petits pois – peas

un poisson – fish

une poissonnerie – fishermonger's

la poitrine – chest, breast

le poivre – pepper

un poivron vert – green pepper

une pomme – apple

une pomme de terre – potato

pommes frites – chips

les pompiers – fire brigade

le pompiste – petrol pump attendant

le porc – pork

un port – port, harbour

une porte – door

un porte-clés – key ring

un porte-feuille – wallet

un porte-monnaie – purse

porter – to wear, carry

   Je porte – I wear, carry

la Poste (P.T.T.) – post office

   code postale – postcode

un poste de secours – first-aid post

un poster – poster

le potage – soup

un pot – pot, jug, can, jar

une poubelle – dustbin

la poudre – powder

une poule – hen

un poulet – chicken

une poupée – doll

pour – for, in order to

un pourboire – tip (waiter)

pourpre – purple

poussez – push (on a door)

la poussière – dust

pouvoir – to be able

pouvez-vous? – can you?

Je peux – I can, I am able

une prairie – meadow

pratique – practical, useful

pratiquer – to practise

   Je pratique – I take part in

préférer – to prefer

   Je préfère – I prefer

premier – first

les premiers soins – first-aid

le prénom – first name

prendre – to take

   Je prends – I take

préparer – to prepare

   Je prépare – I prepare

près (de) – near (to)

pressé – in a rush

   Je suis pressé – I am in a rush

un pressing – dry cleaner's

la pression – pressure

   Bierè à la pression – draught beer

prêt – ready

prêt à porter – ready to wear

prêter – to lend

   Je prête – I lend

   prêtez-moi – lend me

les prévisions météorologiques – weather forecast

le printemps – spring (season)

Printemps – name of well known department store

priorité à droite – give way to the right (road sign)

une prise de courant – (wall) plug, socket

prise de rasoir – razor point

Prisunic – name of well known supermarket/department store

privé – private

le prix – price

prix choc – drastic reductions
prix fixe – fixed price
prix net – net price (everything included)
prochain – next
proche – near
profond – deep
une promenade – walk
promenade à vélo – bicycle ride
se promener – to go for a walk
   Je me promène – I go for a walk
une promotion – promotion, special offer
propre – clean, own
   ma propre voiture – my own car
   une voiture propre – a clean car
le propriétaire – owner
protester – to protest
   Je proteste – I protest
en provenance de – from the direction of
des provisions – provisions, groceries
à proximité – close by, in the locality
la prudence – care, caution
   Soyez prudent! – take care!
une prune – plum
un pruneau – prune, dried plum
puis – then, next
un pull(over) – pullover
un pyjama – pyjamas

un quai – platform
quarante – forty
un quart – quarter
quart d'heure – quarter of an hour

un quartier – district, neighbourhood
quatorze – fourteen
quatre – four
quatrième – fourth
quelque – some, any
quelque chose – something
quelquefois – sometimes
quelque part – somewhere
une queue – tail (animal), queue
   faire la queue – to queue up
une quincaillerie – hardware, ironmonger's shop
quinze – fifteen
quinze jours – a fortnight
quitter – to leave
   Je quitte la maison – I leave the house
quotidien – daily

raccrocher – put the receiver down (phone)
un radiateur – radiator
une radio – a radio
une radiographie – an X-ray
la rage – rabies
raid – stiff, straight
des raisins – grapes
ralentir – to slow down
une randonnée – ramble, hike, road race
un rang – row, line
ranger – to tidy
   Je range – I tidy
rapide – fast
rappel! – caution!
un rasoir – razor
rayé – striped
un rayon – department (shop)
le rayon des disques – record department

la réception – reception
s'adresser à la réception – go to reception
recevoir – to receive
  Je reçois – I receive
une réclamation – a complaint
une réclame – advertisement
une récompense – reward
un reçu – receipt
réduit – reduced
  tarif réduit – reduced price
un réfrigérateur – fridge
regarder – to watch
  Je regarde – I watch
une région – region
un règlement – payment, regulations
regretter – to regret
  Je regrette – I regret
Relais Routier – name of a hotel organisation
rembourser – to refund
  voulez-vous me rembourser? – will you give me my money back?
un remède – cure, remedy
remercier – to thank
  Je vous remercie – I thank you
remplacer – to replace
remplir – to fill
  Je remplis – I fill
  il faut remplir une fiche? – do I have to fill in a form?
un rendez-vous – date, meeting, appointment
rénové – renovated
des renseignements – information
rentrer – to return
  Je rentre – I return
réparer – to repair

  voulez-vous réparer? – will you repair?
un repas – meal
se reposer – to have a rest
  Je me repose – I have a rest
réserver – to reserve
  Je voudrais réserver – I would like to reserve
rester – to stay
  Je reste – I stay
  Je voudrais rester une nuit – I would like to stay for one night
en retard – late
retraité – retired
une réunion – meeting
un réveil – alarm clock
se réveiller – to wake up
  Je me réveille – I wake up
revenir – to come back
  Je reviens – I come back
une revue – magazine
le rez de chaussée – ground floor
le rhum – rum
un rhume – cold (illness)
un rideau – curtain
de rien! – don't mention it!
le riz – rice
une robe – dress
un robinet – tap (sink)
rond – round
un rond-point – roundabout
rose – pink
rosé – rosé (pink)
  vin rosé – rosé wine
une roue – wheel
rouge – red
une route – road
route nationale – main road
roux, rousse – reddish brown, ginger (hair)

le **Royaume Uni** – United Kingdom

une **rue** – street, road

un **sac** – bag
sac de couchage – sleeping bag
sac à dos – rucksack
sac à main – handbag
saignant – rare (steak)
saigner – to bleed
Je saigne – I am bleeding
sain – healthy
sain et sauf – safe and sound
en saison – in season
une **salade** – salad
sale – dirty
salé – salty, savoury
une **salle d'attente** – waiting room
une **salle de bains** – bathroom
une **salle d'eau** – utility/wash room
une **salle à manger** – dining room
une **salle de séjour** – living room
un **salon** – lounge
un **salon d'essayage** – changing room (shop)
salut! – hi!
des **sandales** – sandals
le **sang** – blood
les **sanitaires** – washing facilities
sans – without
sans plomb – lead free (petrol)
santé! – good health!
à votre santé! – good health!
satisfait – satisfied
Je ne suis pas satisfait! – I am not satisfied!
la **sauce** – gravy, sauce
une **saucisse** – sausage
un **saucisson** – sausage
sauf – except

sauf dimanche – except on Sundays
un **saumon** – salmon
le **sauvetage** – rescue, life-saving
ceinture de sauvetage – life-belt
le **savon** – soap
une **séance** – sitting, session
la sèance commence à 8 h. – the performance begins at 8 o'clock
sec – dry
demi-sec – medium dry (wine)
un **séche-cheveux** – hairdrier
un **séchoir** – drier
au secours! – help!
seize – sixteen
le **séjour** – stay
bon séjour – have a good stay (holiday)
le **sel** – salt
un **self** – self service restaurant
une **semaine** – week
le **sens** – direction
sens unique – one way street
sens interdit – no entry
sensass! – great!
un **sentier** – (foot) path
sentir – to smell
ça sent! – it smells!
se sentir – to feel
Je me sens malade – I feel ill
séparé – separated
sept – seven
septembre – September
sérieux – serious
un **serpent** – snake
serré – tight fitting
serrez à droite – keep over to the right (road sign)
une **serrure** – lock
servez-vous – serve youself

les services de garde – emergency services
se servir (de) – to use
Je me sers – I use
service (non) compris – service charge (not) included
une serviette – towel
serviette de table – napkin
le shampooing – shampoo
un short – shorts
S.I. (syndicat d'initiative) – tourist information office
le sirop – fruit squash
six – six
le ski nautique – water skiing
un slip – underpants, swimming trunks
S.N.C.F. (Société Nationale des Chemins de Fer) – French National Railways
une soeur – sister
le soif – thirst
J'ai soif – I am thirsty
le soir – evening
une soirée – an evening (out)
le sol – ground, soil
soldes – sale (department store)
le soleil – sun
le soleil brille – the sun is shining
lever du soleil – sunrise
il fait du soleil – it is sunny
un coup de soleil – sunstroke
Son et Lumière – Sound and Light (show)
sonnez – ring (doorbell)
une sorte (de) – a sort, kind
une sortie – exit
sortie de secours – emergency exit

sortie sans achats – exit without purchase (supermarket)
sortir – to go out
Je sors – I go out
une soucoupe – saucer
souffrant – unwell, in pain, poorly
souffrir – to suffer
Je souffre – I am suffering
la soupe – soup
une souris – mouse
un soul-sol – basement
sous-titré – with subtitles
souterrain – underground
un souvenir – memory, souvenir
souvent – often
le sparadrap – elastoplast
un spectacle – show, play, entertainment
un stade – stadium, sports ground
le standardiste – switchboard operator
une station – holiday resort
station de métro – underground railway station
station-service – petrol station
le stationnement – parking
stationnement interdit – no parking
stationner – to park
le steak frites – steak and chips
un studio – bedsitter
un stylo – pen
le sucre – sugar
le sud – South
ça suffit – that's enough
suivant – following
client suivant – next customer (supermarket)
le super – 4 star petrol
un supplément – extra charge
sur – on

sûr – sure, certain
surgelé – frozen
sus. en sus – extra (charge)
sympa – nice, likeable
le syndicat d'initiative (S.I.) – tourist information office

un tabac – tobacconists
une table – table
un tableau – board, picture
une tache – stain
la taille – size
de taille moyenne – average sized
tant mieux – so much the better
une tante – aunt
un tapis – rug, carpet
un tarif – price list
  demi-tarif – half price
  plein tarif – full (adult) price
  tarif réduit – reduced price
une tarte (aux pommes) – (apple) tart
une tartine – piece of bread and butter
une tasse – cup
une taxe – tax
  hors taxe – duty free
un taxi – taxi
un téléphone – telephone
téléphoner – to telephone
  Je voudrais téléphoner – I would like to make a phone call
la température – temperature
le temps – time, weather
  Je n'ai pas de temps – I have no time
  quel temps fait-il? – what is the weather like?
temps de libre – free time

de temps en temps – from time to time
une tente – tent
  Je peux monter la tente ici? – Can I put my tent up here?
un terrain – piece of land
terrain de sport – sports ground
terrain de camping – campsite
une terrasse – patio, terrace
la terre – ground, earth
la tête – head (body)
le thé – tea
un théâtre – theatre
un timbre – stamp (P.O.)
timide – shy
un tire-bouchon – corkscrew
tirez – pull (door)
le tissu – fabric, material
une toilette – toilet
  où sont les toilettes? – where are the toilets?
une tomate – tomato
un torchon – tea-towel
toujours – always, still
le tourisme – sightseeing
tourner – to turn
  Je tourne – I turn
tousser – to cough
  Je tousse – I cough
tout – all, every
tout confort – very comfortable (hotel)
tout de suite – straight away
tout droit – straight on
toutes directions – all directions (road sign)
une toux – cough
un trajet – journey
une tranche – slice
tranquille – peaceful, quiet
le travail – work, job

travailler — to work
  Je travaille – I work
traverser – to cross
  Je traverse – I cross
treize – thirteen
très – very
un tricot – jumper, jersey
triste – sad, dismal
trois – three
troisième – third
trop – too many, too much
une trousse à crayons – pencil case
trousse de médicaments – first aid kit
trouver – to find
  Je trouve – I find
un tube – tube, a hit record
T.V.A. – V.A.T. (tax)

Uniprix – well known supermarket/department store
unique – sole, only, single
  enfant unique – only child
  sens unique – one way street
utile – useful
utiliser – to use
  J'utilise – I use

les vacances – holidays
  grandes vacances – long holidays
une vache – cow
la vaisselle – plates and dishes, crockery
  faire la vaisselle – to do the washing up
valable – valid
une valise – suitcase
la vanille – vanilla
le vapeur – steam

variable – changeable (weather)
varié – various, varied
le veau – veal
un vélo – bicycle
un vélomoteur – moped
une vendeuse – shop assistant
vendre – to sell
  Je vends – I sell
vendredi – Friday
venir – to come
  Je viens – I come
  venez ici – come here
un vent – wind
une vente – sale
  une salle des ventes – sales-room
le ventre – stomach
un verger – orchard
le verglas – ice on road
vérifier – to check
un verre – glass
verre de vin – glass of wine
vers – towards
vert – green
une veste – coat, (short) jacket
un vestiaire – cloakroom
un veston – jacket (man's)
un vêtement – article of clothing
veuillez – kindly, would you please?
Je veux – I want
la viande – meat
vieux (vieille) – old
un village – village
une ville – town
le vin – wine
vin blanc – white wine
vin rosé – rosé wine
vin rouge – red wine
le vinaigre – vinegar
vingt – twenty

une vingtaine – about twenty
violet – voilet, purple
un virage – bend (on road)
le visage – face
visiter – to visit
  Je visite – I visit
un visiteur – visitor
la vitesse – speed, gears (on car)
une vitrine – shop window
  faire le lèche-vitrine – to go window shopping
voici – here is, this is
une voie – way, road, route, track
voie piétonne – pedestrian precinct
voie sans issue – cul de sac
voilà – there you are
la voile – sailing
  faire la voile – to go sailing
un voisin – neighbour
une voiture – car
le volant – steering wheel, driving seat
un volet – window shutter

un voleur – thief
  au voleur! – stop thief!
vomir – to be sick
  J'ai vomi – I have been sick
(Je) voudrais – I would like
voulez-vous? – will you?
un voyage – trip, journey
  bon voyage – have a good trip
vrai – true, real
vraiment – really
une vue de mer – sea view

le W.C. – toilet
un weekend – weekend

un yaourt – yoghurt
les yeux – the eyes

zéro – nought
une zone bleue – restricted parking area
zoologique (un jardin) – zoo
zut! – bother!

English–French Dictionary

a (an) – un, une
able – compétent(e), capable
  I am able (I can) – Je peux
aboard (a boat) – à bord (de)
about (approximately) – environ, à peu près
above – au-dessus (de)
above all – surtout
abroad – à l'étranger
absolutely – absolument
accelerator – l'accélérateur
accept (to) – accepter
  I accept – j'accepte
accident – un accident
accommodation – un logement, un hébergement
ache (to) – faire mal
  my head aches – j'ai mal à la tête
across (on the other side) – de l'autre côté (de)
activity – une activité
adore (to) – adorer
  I adore – j'adore
adult – un (une) adulte
advertisement – une réclame, la publicité
small ad. – une annonce
aerial – une antenne
aeroplane – un avion
aerosol – un aérosol
afraid (to be) – avoir peur (de)
  I am afraid – j'ai peur
after – après

again – de nouveau, encore une fois
against – contre
age – l'âge (m)
agency – une agence
  travel agency – agence de voyage
  estate agency – agence immobilière
ago, 2 days ago – il y a deux jours
  not long ago – il n'y a pas longtemps
agree (I) – je suis d'accord
agreed (right, okay) – d'accord
aid (first) – les premiers soins (m pl)
ailment – une maladie
air – l'air (m)
  in the open air – en plein air
airbed – un matelas pneumatique
airport – un aéroport
alarm clock – un réveil
alas! – hélas!
all – tout(e)
all day – toute la journée
all night – toute la nuit
allergy – une allergie
allow (to) – permettre
allow me – permettez-moi
almost – presque
alone – seul(e)
already – déjà
also – aussi
always – toujours

a.m. – du matin
amazing – étonnant(e)
ambulance – une ambulance
amiable – aimable
among – parmi
amount – une somme
   quantity – la quantité
amp – un ampère
amuse (oneself) – s'amuser
amusement arcade – une salle de
   jeux
and – et
angry – fâché(e), en colère, furieux,
   furieuse
animal – un animal
aniseed – l'anis (m)
ankle – la cheville
anniversary – un anniversaire
annual – annuel
   (book) – un album
anorak – un anorak
another – un autre, encore un
answer (to) – répondre
answer – une réponse
ant – une fourmi
antibiotic – un antibiotique
antihistomine – un antihis-
   tominique
anxious – anxieux, anxieuse, inquiet
any – des
   have you any? – avez-vous des?
anybody – n'importe qui
anyhow – de toute façon
anything – n'importe quoi
anywhere – n'importe où
apart from – sauf
   every day apart from Sunday
     – tous les jours sauf dimanche
aperitif (drink) – un apéritif
apologize (I) – Je m'excuse

appalling – épouvantable
appetite – l'appétit (m)
apple – une pomme
appliance – un appareil
appreciate (to) – apprécier
apricot – un abricot
apron – un tablier
argument – une dispute
arm – le bras
armchair – un fauteuil
aroma – l'arôme
around – autour
   (about) – environ, vers
arrival – l'arrivée (f)
arrive (to) – arriver
   I arrive – j'arrive
art gallery – un musée d'art, une
   galerie de peinture
artichoke – un artichaut
ash tray – un cendrier
ask (to) – demander
asleep – endormi(e)
asparagus – des asperges (f pl)
assist (to) – aider
assistance – l'aide (f)
at – à
at the butcher's – chez le boucher
attic – un grenier
attitude – l'attitude (f), la manière
August – août
aunt – une tante
autumn – l'automne (m)
average – la moyenne
   of average height – de taille
     moyenne
awkward (clumsy) – gauche
   (embarrassing) – gênant(e)

baby – un bébé
back (body) – le dos
bacon – le lard, le bacon

bad – mauvais(e)
bag – un sac
balcony – un balcon
bald – chauve
ball (large) – un ballon
  (small) – une balle
balloon – un ballon
ballpoint pen – un stylo à bille, un bic
banana – une banane
bandage – un bandage, une bande, un pansement
  crêpe bandage – une bande velpeau
bar – un bar
  (snack) – une buvette
barbecue – un barbecue
barber – un coiffeur
bargain – bon marché, bonne affaire
barn – une grange
barrel – un tonneau
barrier – une barrière
basin – un bol
  washbasin – un lavabo
basket (without handle) – une corbeille
  (with handle) – un panier
bat – une raquette
bath – une baignoire
  to have a bath – prendre un bain
bathe (to) – baigner
bathing costume – un maillot de bain
bathing hat – un bonnet de bain
bathing prohibited – baignade interdite
bathing trunks – un slip
bathroom – la salle de bains
baths – une piscine

battery (car) – une batterie
  (torch) – une pile
be (to) – être
  I am – Je suis
beach – une plage
beautiful – beau, belle
because – parce que
become (to) – devenir
bed – un lit
bee – une abeille
beef – le boeuf
  roast beef – le rosbif
beer – la bière
beetroot – une betterave
before – avant
begin (to) – commencer
  I begin – je commence
behaviour – la conduite
behind – derrière
beige – beige
bell – une cloche
  (on a door) – une sonnette
below (under) – sous, au-dessous de
belt – une ceinture
bench – un banc
beret – un béret
berth – une couchette
beside – à côté de
besides – de plus
best (better) – meilleur
  the best – le mieux
between – entre
bicarbonate (of soda) – bicarbonate de soude
bicycle – un vélo, une bicyclette
big (tall) – grand(e)
  (fat) – gros(se)
bikini – un bikini
bill (café) – l'addition (f)
  (hotel) – la note

(shop) – une facture
bin (dust) – une poubelle
bingo – le loto
bird – un oiseau
biro – un bic
birth – la naissance
  (date of birth) – date de naissance
birthday – l'anniversaire (m)
biscuit – un biscuit
bit (a) – un morceau, un peu
bite (a) – **(insect)** une piqûre
  (dog) – une morsure
bitter (tasting) – amer, amère
black – noir(e)
blade – une lame
blank – blanc, blanche
blanket – une couverture
bleach – l'eau (f) de javel
blind – aveugle
blister (on skin) – une ampoule
block – un bloc
bloke – un type
blond – blond(e)
blood – le sang
blouse – le chemisier
blow (a) – un coup
blow (to) – souffler
blue – bleu(e)
boat – un bateau
body – le corps
boil (to) – bouillir
book (a) – un livre
  (exercise book) – un cahier
book (to) – réserver
boot (car) – le coffre
  (shoe) – une botte
border – la frontière
born – né(e)
borrow (to) – emprunter
boss – le patron

both – tous les deux
bottle – une bouteille
bottom – le fond
  (body) – le derrière
bowels – les intestins (m pl)
bowl – un bol
bowling – un jeu de boules
  (ten pin) – le bowling
box – une boîte
boy – un garçon
boyfriend – un petit ami
bra – un soutien-gorge
bracelet – un bracelet
brake – un frein
  (brake fluid) – le liquide de frein
brand (name) – la marque
  (brand new) – tout neuf
brandy – le cognac
bread – le pain
break (to) – casser, briser
breakfast – le petit déjeuner
breast (chest) – la poitrine
breathalyser – l'alcotest (m)
breathe (to) – respirer
breathing – la respiration
breeze – une brise
bridge – un pont
bright – brillant(e), clair(e)
  (intelligent) – intelligent
  (colour) – vif, vive
bring (to) – apporter
  (person) – amener
Britain – la Grande Bretagne
British – britannique
broad (wide) – large
brochure – un prospectus, un dépliant
bronchitis – la bronchite
broom – un balai
broth – le bouillon

brother – un frère
brown – brun(e)
brown paper – le papier d'emballage
bruise – une contusion
brunette – brune
brush – une brosse
  (to brush one's teeth) – se brosser les dents
bucket – un seau
buckle – une boucle
buffet (food) – un buffet
bug – un insecte
bulb (light) – une ampoule
bull – un taureau
bump (a) – un coup
bun – un petit pain
bungalow – un bungalow
burglar – un cambrioleur
burst (to) – éclater
bush – un buisson
bus stop – un arrêt d'autobus
busy – occupé(e)
  (street) – fréquenté(e)
but – mais
butcher – un boucher
butcher's shop – une boucherie
butter – le beurre
butterfly – un papillon
button – un bouton
buy (to) – acheter
  I buy – j'achète
bye! – au revoir!

cabbage – un chou
cabin – une cabane, une hutte
  (ship) – une cabine
café – un café
cake – un gâteau
calender – un calendrier
call (to) – appeler

I am called – Je m'appelle
calm – calme, tranquille
calor gas – le butane, le butagaz
camera – un appareil (photo)
camp (to) – faire du camping
campbed – un lit de camp
camping – le camping
campsite – un (terrain de) camping
can (to be able) – pouvoir
  I can – Je peux
can – une boîte
cancel (to) – annuler
candle – une bougie
canned – en boîte, conserve
canoe – un canoë
canvas – une toile
cap (for the head) – une casquette
  (for a bottle) – une capsule
car – une voiture
carpark – un parking
carafe (jug) – une carafe
caramel – le caramel
caravan – une caravane
card – une carte
  (birthday card) – une carte d'anniversaire
cardboard – le carton
careful! – attention!
caretaker – un/une concierge, un gardien
carpet – un tapis
  (fitted carpet) – une moquette
carriage (on a train) – une voiture
carry (to) – porter
cartoon – un dessin animé
case (suit) – une valise
cash – l'argent (m) liquide
cash desk – la caisse
cashier – un caissier, une caissière
casserole (food) – le ragoût
  (dish) – une cocotte

cassette – une cassette
castle – un château
catch (to) – attraper
 (catch a bus) – prendre un autobus
cathedral – une cathédrale
cauliflower – un chou-fleur
cautious – prudent(e)
cave – une grotte, une caverne
C.D. player – un lecteur laser
celery – un céleri
cellar (wine) – une cave
chair – une chaise
change (to) – changer
 I change – je change
change (money) – la monnaie
channel (T.V.) – une chaîne
Channel (The English) – la Manche
chat (to) – bavarder
cheap – bon marché, pas cher
check (to) – vérifier
cheek (face) – la joue
cheerio – au revoir
cheese – le fromage
chemist's – une pharmacie
cheque – un chèque
cherry – une cerise
chess – les échecs (m pl)
chest – la poitrine
chicken – un poulet
chicory – une endive
child – un/une enfant
chilly – glacé(e)
chimney – une cheminée
chin – le menton
chips – les frites (f pl)
chives – les ciboulettes (f pl), les civettes (f pl)
chocolate – le chocolat
choice – un choix

choose (to) – choisir
 I choose – je choisis
Christmas – Noël
 (Christmas tree) – un arbre de Noël
 (Father Christmas) – le Père Noël
 (Christmas card) – une carte de Noël
chute – un toboggan
cider – le cidre
cigar – un cigare
cigarette – une cigarette
cinema – le cinéma
circle – un cercle
circus – un cirque
city – une grande ville
clasp (a) – un fermoir
class – une classe
classmate – un/une camarade de classe
classroom – une salle de classe
clean – propre
clean (to) – nettoyer
clear – clair(e)
clear (to) the table – débarrasser la table
clever – habile, intelligent(e)
client – un/une client(e)
cliff – une falaise
climate – le climat
climb (to) – monter, grimper
climbing – l'alpinisme (m)
clinic – une clinique
clock – une pendule
 (large clock) – une horloge
close (to) – fermer
 I close – je ferme
close (nearby) – près (de)
closure – une fermeture
cloth – un tissu

clothes – les vêtements (m pl)
cloud – un nuage
club – un club
coach – un (auto) car
coast – la côte
coat – un manteau
coat hanger – un porte vêtements
cocoa – le cacao
coconut – une noix de coco
cod – un cabillaud, une morue
coffee – le café
coin – une pièce
colander – une passoire à légumes
cold – froid(e)
collar – un col
collect (to) – collectionner
collision – une collision
colour – une couleur
comb – un peigne
come (to) – venir
   I come – je viens
compartment – un compartiment
competition – un concours, une compétition
competitor – un/une concurrent(e)
complain (to) – se plaindre (de)
complaint – une plainte
compulsory – obligatoire
computer – un ordinateur
concert – un concert
conduct (behaviour) – la conduite
congratulations – félicitations
constipation – la constipation
consult (to) – consulter
content (happy) – content(e)
contest – un combat, un concours
continue (to) – continuer
cook (to) – faire la cuisine
cool – frais, fraîche, calme (character)

cop (police) – un flic
cord – une corde
cork – un bouchon
corkscrew – un tire-bouchon
corn – le blé
corner – un coin
cornflower – la farine de maïs
correct – correct(e), exact(e)
corridor – un couloir
cosmetics – les produits (m) de beauté
cost (to) – coûter
   how much does it cost? – ça coûte combien?
costly – cher, chère, coûteux, coûteuse
cot – un lit d'enfant
cottage – une petite maison
cotton – le coton
couch – un canapé, un divan
couchette – une couchette
cough (to) – tousser
   a cough – une toux
counter (shop) – un comptoir
country – un pays
countryside – la campagne
couple – un couple
coupon (advertising) – un bon (réclame)
courgette – une courgette
courtyard – une cour
cousin – un cousin, une cousine
cow – une vache
crab – un crabe
cramp – une crampe
crash – une collision
crayfish – une écrevisse
crayon – un crayon de couleur
crazy – fou, folle
cream – la crème
cress – le cresson

crockery – la vaisselle
cross (a) – une croix
cross (to) – traverser
cross (angry) – fâché(e), en colère
crumb – une miette
cry (to) – pleurer
cucumber – un concombre
culottes – une jupe-culotte
cup – une tasse
currant – un raisin sec
curtain – un rideau
custard – la crème anglaise
customs – la douane
customs officer – un douanier
cut (a) – une coupure
cut (to) – couper
cute – mignon, mignonne
cutlery – les couverts (m pl)
cutlet – une côtelette

dad – papa
daily – tous les jours
daily newspaper – un quotidien
dairy – une crémerie
damage – les dégâts (m pl)
damp – humide
dance (to) – danser
dance (a) – un bal
dark – sombre
date – la date
daughter – une fille
day – un jour
dead – mort, morte
dear – cher, chère
death – la mort
December – décembre
decide (to) – décider
deep – profond(e)
delay – un délai, un retard
delicious – délicieux, délicieuse
dentist – un dentiste

dentures – un dentier
deny (to) – refuser
deposit (part payment) – les arrhes (f pl)
desk – un bureau
dessert – un dessert
diabetes – le diabète
dial (to) – composer le numéro
diarrhoea – la diarrhée
diary – un agenda
dice – un dé
diesel – le gas-oil
difficult – difficile
dine (to) – dîner
dinghy – un canot
dinner (lunch) – le déjeuner
(evening meal) – le dîner
directory (telephone) – un annuaire
disagree (I) – Je ne suis pas d'accord
disappointed – déçu(e)
disaster – une catastrophe
discotheque – une discothèque
discuss (to) – discuter
dish – un plat
dish cloth – un torchon
distance – la distance
   in the distance – dans le lointain
dive (to) – plonger
diversion – une déviation
do (to) – faire
   I do – je fais
doctor – un médecin
dog – un chien
do-it-yourself – le bricolage
donkey – un âne
door – une porte
dormitory – un dortoir
double – double

dozen – une douzaine
draw (to) – dessiner
drawing – le dessin
dress – une robe
dress (to) – s'habiller
  I get dressed – je m'habille
dried – sec, sèche, séché, desséché
drink (to) – boire
  I drink – je bois
drink (a) – une boisson
drive (to) – conduire
driver – un conducteur, un chauffeur
dry – sec, sèche
duck – un canard
duffel bag – un sac marin
dull (boring) – ennuyeux (euse)
  (weather) – gris
during – pendant
dust – la poussière
  to dust – épousseter
duvet – une couette

each – chaque
  ten francs each – dix francs la pièce
ear – une oreille
early – tôt, de bonne heure
  (ahead of time) – en avance
earn (to) – gagner
  I earn – je gagne
earth – la terre
east – l'est (m)
Easter – Pâques (f pl)
easy – facile
eat (to) – manger
  I eat – je mange
edge – le bord
e.g. – par exemple
eiderdown – un édredon
elbow – un coude

elder – aîné(e)
eldest – l'aîné
electric – électrique
eleven – onze
emergency – l'urgence (f)
emery board – une lime à ongles
enclosed (please find) – veuillez trouver ci-joint
end – la fin
end (to) – finir, terminer
engine – un moteur
England – Angleterre (f)
English – anglais(e)
enjoy (to) – aimer
enough – assez
enter (to) – entrer
  I enter – j'entre
entrance – une entrée
envelope – une enveloppe
environment – le milieu, l'environnement (m)
epilepsy – l'épilepsie (f)
error – une erreur
escalator – un escalier roulant
especially – surtout
estate agent's – une agence immobilière
Eurocheque – un eurochèque
evening – le soir, une soirée
example (for) – par exemple
except – sauf
excuse me – excusez-moi, pardon
exhaust (pipe) – un tuyau d'échappement
exhausted – épuisé(e)
exit – une sortie
extra (price) – supplémentaire
eye – un oeil
eyes – les yeux (m pl)

fabric – le tissu

face – le visage
facilities – les installations (f pl), l'équipement (m)
facing – en face (de)
factory – une usine
fair – équitable, juste
fair hair – blond
fair (fun) – une fête (foraine)
fall (to) – tomber
false – faux, fausse
family – une famille
famous – bien connu(e), célèbre
fan belt – une courroie de ventilateur
far – loin
fare (on bus) – le prix du billet
   half fare – demi-tarif
   full fare – plein tarif
farm – une ferme
farther – plus loin
fasten (to) – attacher, fixer, fermer
fast food – le fast food, la restauration rapide
fat – gros, grosse
   (on meat) – le gras
father – le père
father-in-law – le beau-père
fatty (food) – gras, grasse
fault – une faute
favour (help) – un service
   to do a favour – rendre un service
fear – la peur
February – février
fed up (I am) – j'en ai marre
felt – le feutre
felt tip pen – un stylo-feutre
fence – une barrière
ferocious – féroce
ferry – un ferry
festival – une fête

fetch (to) – aller chercher
fête – une fête, une kermesse
fever – une fièvre
few (a) – quelques-uns
fiancé – un fiancé, une fiancée
field – un champ
   (sports) – un terrain
fierce – féroce, sauvage, violent(e)
fifteen – quinze
fifty – cinquante
fill in (to) – remplir
fill it up (petrol tank) – faites le plein
fillet – un filet
fillet steak – le filet de boeuf, le tournedos
film – un film
   (for camera) – une pellicule
film star – une vedette de cinéma
final (last) – dernier, dernière
final (sports) – la finale
find (to) – trouver
fine (weather) – beau
   (very well) – très bien
   (thin) – fin(e)
   (law) – une amende, une contravention
finger – un doigt
finish (to) – finir
   I finish – je finis
finish (the) – la fin
   (end of a race) – l'arrivée (f)
fire – un feu, un incendie
fire brigade – les pompiers (m pl)
first – premier, première
   (first of all) – d'abord
fish – un poisson
fit (in good shape) – en bonne forme
fitted (kitchen) – (cuisine) équipée, aménagée

five – cinq
fix (to) – réparer
flag – un drapeau
  (stone) – une dalle
flame – une flamme
flammable – inflammable
flannel (face) – un gant de toilette
flash (news) – un flash d'information
  (lightning) – un éclair
flask (vacuum) – un thermos
flat – plat
  (tyre) – dégonflé
  (house) – un appartement
flavour – le parfum
flight – un vol
flippers (swimming) – les palmes (f pl)
float (to) – flotter
floor – un plancher, le sol
  (storey) – un étage
floor (first) – le premier étage
floor (ground) – le rez de chaussée
flour – la farine
flower – une fleur
flu – la grippe
fluently – couramment
fluid – le fluide
fly (insect) – une mouche
fly (to) – voler
fog – le brouillard
fold (to) – plier
follow (to) – suivre
food – la nourriture
  (groceries) – l'alimentation (f)
fool – un idiot, une idiote
foolish – stupide, imprudent(e)
foot – un pied
  on foot – à pied
for – pour
forbidden – interdit(e), défendu(e)

forecast (weather) – une prévision météorologique
forehead – le front
foreign – étranger, étrangère
forest – une forêt
forget (to) – oublier
fork – une fourchette
fortnight – quinze jours (m pl), deux semaines (f pl)
fortunate – heureux, heureuse
fortune (luck) – la chance
  (wealth) – une fortune
forward (ahead of schedule) – en avance
  (movement) – en avant
  (not shy) – direct, ouvert
fountain – une fontaine
fountain pen – un stylo à encre
four – quatre
fowl – la volaille
fracture – une fracture
fragile – fragile
France – la France
free – libre
  (of charge) – gratuit(e)
freeze (to) – geler
  it is freezing – il gèle
freezing (cold) – glacial(e)
French – français(e)
frequent – fréquent(e)
fresh – frais, fraîche
  (new) – nouveau, nouvelle
Friday – vendredi
fridge – un frigo, un frigidaire
fried – frit(e)
fried egg – un oeuf sur le plat
friend – un ami, une amie
friendly – amical(e), gentil(le)
friendship – l'amitié (f)
fritter – un beignet
frog – une grenouille

frogs' legs – des cuisses (f) de grenouille

from – de

  (from a certain time onwards) – à partir de

front – le devant

  in front of – devant

front door – une porte d'entrée

frost – le gel, la gelée, le givre

froth – la mousse

fruit – le fruit

fruit shop – une fruiterie

frying pan – une poêle

fuel (car) – le carburant

  fuel tank – un réservoir

full – plein(e)

fun – l'amusement, un divertissement

  (to have fun) – s'amuser

fun fair – une fête (foraine)

funny – amusant(e), drôle

  (strange) – curieux, curieuse, bizarre

fur – la fourrure

furious – furieux, furieuse

furniture – les meubles (m pl)

further (distance) – plus loin

fuse – un fusible

future – futur(e)

  the future – l'avenir (m)

gale – une rafale de vent

game – un jeu, un match

garage – un garage

garden – un jardin

garlic – l'ail (m)

garment – un vêtement

gas – le gaz

  (petrol) – l'essence (f)

gas cylinder – une bouteille de gaz

gas fire – un radiateur à gaz

gasket (on a car) – un joint de culasse

gassy – gazeux, gazeuse

gate (garden) – un portail

  (farm) – une barrière

gear (car) – une vitesse

  (equipment) – l'équipement (m), le matériel

generous – généreux, généreuse

  (large amount) – copieux, copieuse

gentle – doux, douce

gentleman – un monsieur

gently – doucement

gents' (toilet) – W.C. pour hommes

genuine – véritable, authentique, sincère

geography – la géographie

germ – un microbe

German – allemand(e)

Germany – l'Allemagne (f)

get (to) (obtain) – obtenir

  (receive) – recevoir

  (catch a bus) – prendre

get up (to) – se lever

  I get up – je me lève

giant – un géant

gift – un cadeau

girl – une fille, une fillette, une jeune fille

give (to) – donner

  I give – je donne

  give me – donnez-moi

glad – content(e)

gladly – volontiers

glass – un verre

looking glass – un miroir

glasses (spectacles) – des lunettes (f pl)

glove – un gant

glue – la colle
glue (to) – coller
go (to) – aller
  I go – je vais
  go away (to) – partir
  go back (to) – rentrer, retourner, revenir
  go by (to) – passer
  go down (to) – descendre
  I go down – je descends
  go for (to) – aller chercher
  go in (to) – entrer
  I go in – j'entre
  go on (to) – continuer
  go out (to) – sortir
  I go out – je sors
goal (in sport) – un but
God – Dieu (m)
  My God! – Mon Dieu!
gold – l'or (m)
  made of gold – en or
goldfish – un poisson rouge
good – bon, bonne
  (kind) – gentil, gentille
  (child's behaviour) – sage
  very good – très bien
goose – une oie
gooseberry – une groseille
gorgeous – splendide, superbe
grand – magnifique, splendide
grandchild – un petit-enfant, une petite-enfant
grandfather – un grand-père
grandmother – une grand-mère
grandson – un petit-fils
granddaughter – une petite-fille
grape – un raisin
grapefruit – un pamplemousse
grass – l'herbe (f)
grateful – reconnaissant(e)
gravy – la sauce

graze (injury) – une écorchure
grease – la graisse
  grease (to) – graisser
grease-proof paper – le papier sulfurisé
greasy – gras, grasse, graisseux, graisseuse
great – grand(e) (**large**), formidable (**super**)
Great Britain – la Grande Bretagne
green – vert(e)
greet (to) – accueillir
greeting – une salutation
greetings card – une carte de voeux
grey – gris(e)
  (dismal) – sombre
grill – un gril
  to grill – griller
  grilled – grillé(e)
grim – sinistre, lugubre
grimy – crasseux, crasseuse
grocer's – une épicerie
groceries – les provisions (f pl)
ground – le sol, la terre
  on the ground – par terre
ground floor – le rez-de-chaussée
groundsheet – un tapis de sol
group – un groupe
  school group – un groupe scolaire
grow (to) (plants) – pousser, cultiver
  (person) – grandir
  (increase) – augmenter
guarantee – une garantie
guest – un invité, une invitée
  (in a hotel) – un client, une cliente
guestroom – une chambre d'amis

guide (a) – un guide (**also guide book**)
guitar – une guitare
gull (sea) – une mouette
gun – un revolver; un pistolet
guy (man) – un type
gymnasium – un gymnase
gymshoes – les chaussures (f pl) de gymnastique

hail(stone) – la grêle
hair – les cheveux (m pl)
hairbrush – une brosse à cheveux
hairdresser – un coiffeur, une coiffeuse
hairdrier – un sèche-cheveux
hairpin – une épingle à cheveux
half – la moitié, demi(e)
half hour – une demi-heure
half a dozen – une demi-douzaine
half price – à moitié prix
hall – une salle
  (entrance) – une entrée
ham – le jambon
hamburger – un hamburger
hammer – un marteau
hammock – un hamac
hamster – un hamster
hand – la main
  left hand – la main gauche
  right hand – la main droite
handbag – un sac à main
handkerchief – un mouchoir
handle – une poignée
handsome – beau, belle
handwriting – l'écriture (f)
hang-gliding – le vol libre, le vol sur aile delta
happy – heureux, heureuse
Happy Birthday! – Bon anniversaire!

harbour – le port
hard – dur(e), difficile
hardware (shop) – une quincaillerie
hare – un lièvre
harsh – dur(e), sévère
harvest – la moisson
  (of grapes) – la vendange
  (of fruit) – la récolte
hash – le hachis
haste – la hâte
hastily – à la hâte
hate (to) – détester
  I hate – je déteste
have (to) – avoir
  I have – j'ai
  have you? – avez-vous?
haversack – un sac à dos
hay – le foin
hay fever – un rhume des foins
hazard warning lights – les feux (f pl) de détresse
he – il
head – la tête
health – la santé
healthy – en bonne santé
hear (to) – entendre
  I hear – j'entends
heart – le coeur
heart attack – une crise cardiaque
hearth – un foyer, une cheminée
heat – la chaleur
  to heat – chauffer
heat stroke – un coup de chaleur
heating (central) – le chauffage central
heatwave – une vague de chaleur
heavy – lourd(e)
hedgehog – un hérisson
heel – un talon

height (of person) – la taille, la grandeur

(of object) – la hauteur

(of aeroplane) – l'altitude (f)

helicopter – un hélicoptère

hello – bonjour, salut

helmet – un casque

help – l'aide (f)

help! – au secours!

to help – aider

I help – j'aide

can I help you? – Je peux vous aider?

can you help me? – vous pouvez m'aider?

help yourself – servez-vous

hen – une poule

herb – une herbe

here – ici

here is (or are) – voici

near here – près d'ici

hi! – salut!

hide (to) – cacher

hide and seek – le cache-cache

high – haut(e)

high street – la grande rue

highway – une grand'route

highway code – le code de la route

hike – une excursion à pied, une randonnée

to go for a hike – faire une randonnée

hill – une colline

hip – la hanche

hire – la location

to hire – louer

can I hire? – Je peux louer?

history – l'histoire (f)

hit (to) – frapper, cogner, entrer en collision avec, heurter

hitch-hiking – l'autostop (m)

hobby – un passetemps

hold (to) – tenir

I hold – je tiens

hole – un trou

holiday – les vacances (f pl)

(day off) – un jour de congé

(public) – un jour férié

holiday camp – une colonie de vacances

holiday resort – un centre de vacances, une station

home – la maison

at (my) home – chez moi

to go home – rentrer à la maison

home address – le domicile habituel

home made – maison

homework – les devoirs (m pl)

honest – honnête

(sincere) – franc, franche

honestly – franchement

honey – le miel

hook (fishing) – un hameçon

hooligan – un voyou

hoover – un aspirateur

to hoover – passer l'aspirateur

hope (to) – espérer

I hope – j'espère

horoscope – un horoscope

horrible – horrible, affreux, affreuse

horse – un cheval

horses – des chevaux

to go horse riding – faire de l'équitation

hospitable – hospitalier, hospitalière

hospital – un hôpital

hostel (youth) – une auberge de jeunesse

hot – chaud(e)
hot water – l'eau (f) chaude
hour – une heure
  at any hour – à toute heure
hourly – toutes les heures
house – une maison
housework (to do) – faire le ménage
hovercraft – un aéroglisseur
how – comment
how are you? – comment ça va?
how many/much? – combien?
huge – énorme, immense
hunger – la faim
hungry (I am) – j'ai faim
hurry (to) – se dépêcher
hurry up! – dépêchez-vous!
hurt (injured) – blessé(e)
  that hurts! – ça fait mal!
husband – le mari
hut – une hutte
  (shed) – une cabane
hypermarket – un hypermarché

I – je
I am – je suis
ice – la glace
ice cream – une glace
ice rink – une patinoire
ice skating – le patinage à glace
icy (temperature) – glacial(e)
idea – une idée
  good idea – bonne idée
identity card – une carte d'identité
idiot – un idiot, une idiote, un/une imbécile
idle – paresseux, paresseuse
if – si
ignition – le contact
ignition key – une clé de contact
ill – malade

illness – une maladie
immediately – immédiatement
impatient – impatient(e)
important – important(e)
impossible – impossible
improve (to) – améliorer
improvement – une amélioration
in – dans
including – y compris
inconvenient – malcommode
incorrect – incorrect(e), inexact(e)
increase (to) – augmenter
  an increase – une augmentation
indeed – en effet
  yes indeed! – certainement
indoors – à l'intérieur
inexpensive – bon marché
infant – un petit enfant, une petite enfant
infection – une infection
infectious – contagieux, contagieuse
infirmary – un hôpital
inflammable – inflammable
influenza – la grippe
information – l'information (f), les renseignements (m pl)
information office – un bureau de renseignements
inhabitant – un habitant
injection – une piqûre
injure (to) – blesser
injured – blessé(e)
injury (an) – une blessure
ink – l'encre (f)
in-laws – les beaux-parents (m pl)
inn – une auberge
in-patient – un/une malade hospitalisé(e)
insect – un insecte
inside – à l'intérieur

inside out – à l'envers
instant – un instant
instant coffee – le café instantané
instantly – tout de suite
instead of – au lieu de
insurance – l'assurance (f)
interest (to show) in – s'intéresser à
    I am interested in – je m'intéresse à
interested – intéressé(e)
interesting – intéressant(e)
intermission (theatre) – l'entr'acte (m)
interval (sport) – la mi-temps
intolerable – insupportable
invite (to) – inviter
    I invite you – je t'invite
invoice – une facture
iron – un fer
    (for clothes) – un fer à repasser
    to iron clothes – repasser les vêtements
ironmonger's – une quincaillerie
island – une île
Italian – italien(ne)
Italy – l'Italie (f)
itinerary – l'itinéraire (m)

jack (for car) – un cric
jacket – une veste, un veston
jam – la confiture
    traffic jam – un embouteillage
January – janvier
jar – un pot, un bocal
jeans – un blue-jean
jelly – la gelée
jersey – un tricot
jigsaw – un puzzle
job – un travail, un emploi, un poste

jobless – sans travail, au chômage
jogging – le footing
joke – une plaisanterie
    to joke – plaisanter
journey – un voyage
    (distance covered) – le trajet
jug – un pot, une cruche
juice (fruit) – le jus de fruit
July – juillet
jump (to) – sauter
jumper – un pullover
jump leads (for car) – les câbles (m pl) de démarrage
junction – un carrefour
June – juin
junk – le bric à brac
junk food – les snacks (m pl)
just – juste
just in time – juste à temps

keen (eager) – plein(e) d'enthousiasme
keep (to) – garder
keep fit – la gymnastique de maintien
keepsake – un souvenir
kettle – une bouilloire
key – une clé
keyboard – un clavier (électronique)
keyring – un porte-clés
kid (slang) – un gamin, une gamine, un/une gosse
kidney – un rognon
kilo – un kilo
kilogram – un kilogramme
kilometre – un kilomètre
kind – gentil(le), aimable
    (sort) – une sorte
    (species) – un genre
kindergarten – un jardin d'enfants

kindness – la bonté, la gentillesse
kipper – un hareng fumé et salé
kiss (a) – un baiser
   to kiss – embrasser
kitchen – une cuisine
knee – un genou
knickers – une culotte de femme
knife – un couteau
   penknife – un canif
knock (to) – frapper
knot – un noeud
know (to) – savoir
   I know – je sais
   to know a person or place –
   connaître
   I know – je connais

label – une étiquette
lace (shoe) – un lacet
lad – un gars, un garçon
ladder – une échelle
lady – une dame
lager – la bière blonde
lake – un lac
lamb – un agneau
lamp – une lampe
land (country) – un pays
   (as opposed to sea) – la terre
   (soil) – la terre, le terrain
landscape – le paysage
lane – un chemin
   (in town) – une ruelle
language – une langue
lanky – grand(e) et maigre
large – grand(e), gros(se)
last (not first) – dernier, dernière
last week – la semaine dernière
last (to) – durer
   it lasts – ça dure
late (not on time) – en retard
   (at a late hour) – tard

later – plus tard
laugh (to) – rire
   I laugh – je ris
launderette – une laverie
laundry – une blanchisserie
lawn – une pelouse
laxative – un laxatif
lazy – paresseux, paresseuse
leaf – une feuille
least (the) – le plus petit, le moin-
   dre
leave (to) (depart) – partir
   I leave – je pars
   (go away from) – quitter
   I leave – je quitte
leek – un poireau
left (on the, to the) – à gauche
left-luggage office – la consigne
leg – la jambe
   chicken leg – une cuisse de
   poulet
leisure – le loisir, le temps libre
leisure centre – un centre de
   loisirs
lemon – un citron
lend (to) – prêter
lend me – prêtez-moi
length – la longueur
lens (of camera) – l'objectif (m)
less – moins (de)
lesson – un cours, une leçon
let (to) (allow) – laisser
   let me pass – laissez-moi passer
   (to hire) – louer
letter – une lettre
lettuce – une laitue
library – une bibliothèque
licence – une autorisation, un permis
life – la vie

lifeguard – un surveillant de baignade

lifejacket – un gilet (or une ceinture) de sauvetage

light – une lumière, une lampe
　(colour) – clair(e)

lightbulb – une ampoule

lighter (cigarette) – un briquet

lighthouse – un phare

lightning – un éclair, la foudre

like (to) – aimer
　I like – j'aime
　I would like – je voudrais
　(similar) – semblable, pareil(le)

likeable – sympathique, agréable

lime – un citron vert, une lime

line – une ligne

linen – le linge

lip – une lèvre

liquid – le liquide

list – une liste

listen (to) – écouter
　I listen – j'écoute

litter – les ordures (f pl)

little – petit(e)
　(not much) – peu
　(very little) – très peu

loaf – un pain

loan (a) – un prêt
　to loan – louer

lobster – un homard

lock (a) – une serrure
　to lock – fermer à clé

loft – un grenier

lollipop – une sucette

London – Londres

lonely – seul(e), solitaire, isolé(e)

long – long, longue
　a long time – longtemps

loo – le W.C

look (to) – regarder

I look – je regarde
(seem) – sembler
(look for) – chercher
(look after) – s'occuper (de)
(look forward to) – attendre avec impatience

lorry – un camion

loss – la perte

lost – perdu(e)

lost and found – les objets trouvés

lot (a) of – beaucoup (de)

loud – bruyant(e), sonore, fort(e)

loudspeaker – un haut-parleur

lousy (awful) – moche

love – l'amour (m)
　to love – aimer, adorer
　to be in love with someone – être amoureux de quelqu'un

lovely – (très) joli(e), ravissant(e), charmant(e), agréable

low – bas, basse

luck – la chance
　good luck! – bonne chance!

luckily – heureusement

luggage – les bagages (m pl)

luggage rack (on car) – une galerie

lukewarm – tiède

lump (swelling) – une grosseur

lunch – le déjeuner

lung – un poumon

luxurious – luxueux, luxueuse

luxury – le luxe

mac – un imperméable

madam – madame

made of – fait en

magazine – un magazine, une revue

magnificent – magnifique

mail – la poste

(letters) – le courrier
main – principal(e)
maize – le maïs
make (to) – faire
  I make – je fais
male – mâle, masculin
man – un homme
gentleman – un monsieur
manage (to) – se débrouiller
  I am managing well – je me débrouille bien
man-made – artificiel(le)
manner – la manière, la façon
many – beaucoup (de)
map – une carte
March – mars
margarine – la margarine
market – le marché
  flea market – un marché aux puces
  supermarket – un supermarché
market place – la place du marché
marmalade – la confiture d'oranges
marriage – le mariage
married – marié(e)
marry (to) – épouser, se marier avec
mashed (potato) – la purée de pommes de terre
massive – énorme, massif, massive
match (for lighting) – une allumette
  (game) – un match, une partie
mate (friend) – un copain, une copine
material (cloth) – le tissu
maths – les mathématiques (f pl)
mattress – un matelas
May – mai
meal – un repas

meal time – l'heure du repas
mean (with money) – avare
  what do you mean? – que voulez-vous dire?
measure (to) – mesurer
  (ruler) – une règle
meat – la viande
mechanic – un mécanicien
medicine – un médicament
medium (sized) – moyen(ne)
meet (to) – rencontrer
  (by arrangement) – retrouver
  (for the first time) – faire la connaissance (de)
meeting (a) – une rencontre, une réunion
  (appointment) – un rendez-vous
melon – un melon
member – un membre
membership card – une carte de membre, une carte d'adhérent
memory – la mémoire, un souvenir
mend (to) – réparer
menu – un menu
  (printed) – une carte
merchant – un négociant, un marchand
mess – le désordre
message – un message
messy – sale, en désordre
metre – un mètre
microwave – un four à micro-ondes
middle – le milieu
midnight – minuit (m)
might (may) (I) – je pourrais
mild – doux, douce
milk – le lait
mill – un moulin

(**factory**) – une usine, une fabrique

million – un million

mince (meat) – la viande hâchée

mind (look after) to – garder, s'occuper de, soigner

mineral water – l'eau (f) minérale

minibus – un minibus

miniskirt – une mini-jupe

mint – la menthe

minus – moins

minute – une minute

mirror – un miroir, une glace

mishap – une mésaventure

missing – disparu(e)

mistake – une erreur, une faute

   to make a mistake – faire une erreur

mister – monsieur

mistress – une maîtresse

   (**primary school mistress**) – une institutrice

mix (to) – mélanger

mobile home – une caravane

modern – moderne

modest – modeste

moist – humide

moment (at the) – à ce moment

Monday – lundi

money – l'argent (m)

month – un mois

monument – un monument

mood – l'humeur (f), la disposition

   in a good/bad mood – de bonne/mauvaise humeur

moon – la lune

mop (a) – un balai à laver

   to mop – éponger, essuyer

moped – un cyclomoteur, un vélo-moteur

more – plus (de)

(**additional**) – encore (de)

more wine, please – encore de vin, s'il vous plaît

morning – le matin, la matinée

   seven o'clock in the morning – sept heures du matin

mosquito – un moustique

most – la plupart (de)

mostly – surtout, principalement

motel – un motel

moth – un papillon de nuit

mother – la mère

motor – un moteur

motorbike – une moto

motorboat – un bateau moteur

motorcar – une automobile, une voiture

motorist – un/une automobiliste

motorway – une autoroute

mountain – une montagne

mountaineer – un/une alpiniste

mountaineering – l'alpinisme (m)

mountainous – montagneux, montagneuse

mouse – une souris

moustache – les moustaches (f pl)

mouth – la bouche

   (**of animal**) – la gueule

move (in a game) – un coup

   (**your turn to play**) – un tour

   (**change of house**) – le déménagement

   move (to) – déplacer, bouger

   to move house – déménager

movement – un mouvement

Mr – monsieur

Mrs – madame

Ms (Miss or Mrs) – madame

much – beaucoup (de)

   how much? – combien?

   too much – trop (de)

as much as – autant de
muck (mud) – la boue
mug – une grande tasse
mum, mummy – maman
museum – un musée
mushroom – un champignon
music – la musique
mussel – une moule
must (I) – je dois, il me faut
mustard – la moutarde
mutton – le mouton
my – mon (m), ma (f), mes (pl)
myself – moi-même

name – un nom
　surname – le nom de famille
　first name – le prénom
nanny – une bonne d'enfants
napkin – une serviette de table
narrow – étroit(e)
nasty – méchant(e), désagréable,
　dégoûtant(e), mauvais(e)
natural – naturel(le)
naturally – naturellement
nature – la nature
nausea – la naussée
near – près (de), proche
neat – soigné(e)
　(room) – bien rangé(e)
necessary – nécessaire
　it is necessary – il faut
neck – le cou
necklace – un collier
necktie – une cravate
need (to) – avoir besoin (de)
　I need – j'ai besoin de, il me
　　faut
needle – une aiguille
neighbour – un voisin, une voisine
neither . . . nor – ni . . . ni
nephew – un neveu

nerve – un nerf
　(courage) – le courage
nervous – nerveux, nerveuse, in-
　quiet, inquiète
nest – un nid
net – un filet
netball – le netball
nettle – une ortie
neutral – neutre
never – ne . . . jamais
new – nouveau, nouvelle
　brand new – neuf, neuve
news – les nouvelles (f pl)
　(T.V.) – les informations (f pl),
　　les actualités (f pl)
New Year – le Nouvel An
New Year's Day – le Jour de l'An
next – prochain(e)
　(following) – suivant(e)
next time – la prochaine fois
next day – le lendemain
next year – l'année prochaine
nice (person) – sympathique,
　agréable, gentil(le)
nice looking – joli(e), beau, belle
nickname – un surnom
niece – une nièce
night – la nuit
　(evening) – le soir
nightclub – une boîte de nuit
nightdress – une chemise de nuit
night life – la vie nocturne
nightly – chaque nuit
nightmare – un cauchemar
nil – rien (m), zéro (m)
nimble – agile
nine – neuf
no – non
nobody – ne . . . personne
noise – un bruit
none – aucun(e)

non smoker – non fumeur
noodles – les nouilles (f pl)
noon – midi (m)
normal – normal(e)
normally – normalement
Normandy – la Normandie
north – le nord
north-west – le nord-ouest
north-east – le nord-est
nose – le nez
not – (ne) . . . pas
not at all – pas du tout
note – une note
    (letter) – un mot
    banknote – un billet de banque
note paper – le papier à lettres
nothing – (ne) . . . rien
notice (a) – un avis
    to notice – remarquer
noticeboard – un panneau d'affichage
notify (to) – notifier
nought – zéro (m)
November – novembre
now – maintenant, en ce moment
    right now – tout de suite
now and then – de temps en temps
nowadays – de nos jours
nowhere – nulle part
nuisance (it's a) – c'est très ennuyeux
number – un nombre
    (numeral) – un chiffre
    (of house, car, telephone) – le numéro
number plate (of car) – une plaque d'immatriculation
numerous – nombreux, nombreuse
nurse – une infirmière

nursery (school) – une école maternelle
nut – une noix, une noisette
nutmeg – une muscade
nylon – le nylon

object – un objet
obliged (to be) to – être obligé(e) de
obnoxious – odieux, odieuse
observe (to) – observer
obviously – bien sûr
occupation – un métier, une profession
occupied – occupé(e)
o'clock (it is 5 o'clock) – il est cinq heures
October – octobre
odd – bizarre
odour – une odeur
of – de
offer (to) – offrir
office – un bureau
office worker – employé(e) de bureau
often – souvent
oh! – oh! ah!
oil – l'huile (f)
    (for central heating) – le mazout
okay – d'accord
    are you okay? – ça va?
old – vieux, vieille, âgé(e)
    (former) – ancien, ancienne
olive – une olive
olive oil – l'huile d'olive
omelette – une omelette
on – sur
on holiday – en vacances
on Friday – vendredi
once – une fois

(at one time in the past) – autrefois

one – un, une

only – seulement

  only child – enfant unique

  not only, but also – non seulement, mais aussi

open (to) – ouvrir

  I open – j'ouvre

  open (not closed) – ouvert(e)

opening (an) – une ouverture

operation – une opération

  (of machine) – le fonctionnement

operator (telephone) – un/une téléphoniste

  switchboard operator – un/une standardiste

opinion – une opinion, un avis

  in my opinion – à mon avis

opportunity – une occasion

opposite – en face (de)

optician – un opticien, une opticienne

or – ou

or else – ou bien

orange – une orange

orange juice – le jus d'orange

orchard – un verger

orchestra – un orchestre

order – un ordre, une commande

order (to) a meal – commander

ordinary – ordinaire, normal(e)

  out of the ordinary – exceptionnel(le)

other – autre

other than or except for – sauf

otherwise – autrement

ouch! – aïe!

ought to (I) – je devrais

our – notre (singular), nos (plural)

out – dehors

out of petrol – en panne d'essence

out of order – en panne

outboard motor – un moteur hors-bord

outdoors – en plein air

out of date (clothes) – démodé(e)

outside – l'extérieur (m), dehors, à l'extérieur

outsize (clothes) – grande taille (f)

outstanding – exceptionnel(le)

oval – oval(e)

oven – un four

over (finished) – fini(e), terminé(e)

  (above) – au-dessus (de)

  over there – là-bas

  all over – partout

overseas (abroad) – à l'étranger

owe (to) – devoir

  how much do I owe you? – je vous dois combien?

owl – un hibou

own (to) – posséder

  my own room – ma propre chambre

  on my own – tout(e) seul(e)

oyster – une huître

pack (to) – faire ses bagages

package – un paquet

package tour – un voyage organisé

packed lunch – un repas froid

packet – un paquet

pad – un bloc (notes)

paddling pool – un petit bassin

page – une page

pain – une douleur

  I am in pain – je souffre, j'ai mal

painful – douloureux, douloureuse
painkiller – un calmant
paint – la peinture
  to paint – peindre
painting (a) – une peinture, un tableau
pair – une paire
pal – un copain, une copine
pale – pâle
pamphlet – une brochure
pan – une casserole
  frying pan – une poêle
pancake – une crêpe
panic – la panique
pantihose – un collant
pants (trousers) – un pantalon
paper – le papier
  wallpaper – le papier peint
  newspaper – un journal
paper handkerchief – un mouchoir en papier
parasol – une ombrelle
parcel – un paquet, un colis
pardon (me)! – excusez-moi!
  I beg your pardon – Je suis désolé(e)
park – un jardin public, un parc
  to park – garer, stationner
  car park – un parking
parking – le stationnement
  no parking – stationnement interdit
parking meter – un parcomètre
parsley – le persil
parsnip – un panais
part – une partie
  to take part in – participer à
  for my part – en ce qui me concerne
particpate in (to) – participer à

part-time – à mi-temps, à temps partiel
party – une réception, une soirée, une fête, une boum
pass (to) – passer
  (an exam) – réussir
passage – un couloir
  (by boat) – une traversée
passenger – un passager, une passagère
passer-by – un passant, une passante
passport – un passeport
past (further than) – plus loin que
  (later than) – après
pasta – les pâtes (f pl)
pastille – une pastille
pastime – un passetemps, une distraction
pastry (cake) – une pâtisserie
pâté – le pâté, la terrine
path – un chemin, un sentier, une allée
patient – patient(e)
patient (a) – un/une malade
pay (to) – payer
  to pay a bill – régler
peace – la paix, le calme, la tranquillité
peaceful – paisible, calme
peach – une pêche
peanut – une cacahuète
pear – une poire
pedestrian – un piéton
peg (clothes) – une pince à linge
pen – un stylo
pencil – un crayon
penfriend – un correspondant, une correspondante
penknife – un canif

people – des gens (m pl), des personnes (f pl)

pepper – le poivre
  (vegetable) – un poivron

per cent – pour cent

percolator – une cafetière électrique

perfect – parfait(e)

perfume – le parfum

perhaps – peut-être

permission – la permission, l'autorisation (f)

person – une personne

personally – personnellement

pet – un animal familier

petrol – l'essence (f)

petrol pump – une pompe à essence

petrol station – une station-service

petrol tank – un réservoir d'essence

pheasant – un faisan

phone – un téléphone
  to phone – téléphoner

photo – une photo(graphie)

physics – la physique

piano – un piano

picnic – un pique-nique

picture – un tableau, une image

picturesque – pittoresque

pie (meat) – un pâté en croûte

piece – un morceau

pig – un cochon

pigeon – un pigeon

pill – une pilule

pillow – un oreiller

pimple – un bouton

pin – une épingle

pineapple – un ananas

pipe – une pipe

pitch (on a campsite) – un emplacement

pizza – une pizza

place – un endroit, un lieu, une place
  to place – placer, mettre

plaice – un carrelet

plain (without seasoning or flavour) – nature
  (clear) – clair(e), évident(e)

plan – un plan
  (scheme) – un projet
  to plan – organiser

plaster (sticking) – un pansement (adhésif), un sparadrap

plastic – le plastique
  made of plastic – en plastique

plate – une assiette

play (to) – jouer
  I play – je joue
  play (theatre) – une pièce

player – une joueur

playground – une cour de récréation

playing field – un terrain de sport

pleasant – agréable

please – s'il te plaît (familiar), s'il vous plaît (formal)

pleased – content(e)

pleasing – plaisant(e)

pleasure – un plaisir
  it's a pleasure – je vous en prie

plenty – beaucoup (de)

plug (sink) – un bouchon
  electric plug – une prise de courant

plum – une prune

plumber – un plombier

plump – dodu(e)

p.m. – de l'après-midi

pocket – une poche

pocket money – l'argent (m) de poche
police – la police
policeman – un agent de police
police station – le commissariat
polite – poli(e)
pond – un étang
pony – un poney
pool (pond) – une mare
  (artificial) – un bassin
  (swimming pool) – une piscine
poor – pauvre
pork – le porc
port (harbour) – un port
  (wine from Portugal) – le porto
portable – portatif, portative
possible – possible
post (collection) – la levée
  (letters) – le courrier
  (job) – un poste
  (pole) – un poteau
  to post a letter – poster
postbox – une boîte aux lettres
postcard – une carte postale
postcode – un code postale
postman – un facteur
post office – la poste
poster – une affiche
pot (cooking) – une marmite, une casserole
  (for plants, jam) – un pot
potato – une pomme de terre
potted – en conserve
poultry – la volaille
pound – une livre, un demi-kilo
  (money) – une livre sterling, une livre anglaise
pour (to) – verser
powder – la poudre
power (electric) – le courant

practical – pratique
practise (to) – s'exercer à
  (to train) – pratiquer
pram – une voiture d'enfant
prawn – une crevette
precinct (pedestrian) – une zone piétonnière
prefer (to) – préférer
  I prefer – je préfère
prepare (to) – préparer
prescription – une ordonnance
present – un cadeau
press (to) (clothes) – repasser
pretty – joli(e)
prevent (to) – empêcher
price – le prix
price list – une liste des prix
print (to) – imprimer
  (publish) – publier
private – privé(e)
prize – un prix
problem – un problème
product – un produit
profession – une profession
programme – un programme
  (TV/radio) – une émission
promise – une promesse
  to promise – promettre
  I promise – je promets
property – une propriété
proud – fier, fière
public transport – les transports (m pl) en commun
pudding – un dessert
  black pudding – un boudin noir
pull (to) – tirer
  (on a door) – tirez
pullover – un pull(over)
puncture – une crevaison
pupil (school) – un/une élève
pure – pur(e)

purple – violet(te), pourpre
purse – un porte-monnaie
push (to) – pousser
  (on a door) – poussez
put (to) – mettre
  I put – je mets
put on (clothes) – mettre
  I put on – je mets
pyjamas – un pyjama

quality – la qualité
quarrel – une dispute
  to quarrel – se disputer
quarter – un quart
quarter of an hour – un quart
  d'heure
quay – un quai
question – une question
queue – une queue, une file
  to queue up – faire la queue
quick – vite
quiet – tranquille, calme
quietly – tranquillement
quilt – un édredon
quite – assez, plutôt
quite so! – exactement!

rabbit – un lapin
rabies – la rage
race (competition) – une course
  to race – faire la course
racket (tennis) – une raquette
radiator – un radiateur
radio – une radio
  on the radio – à la radio
radish – un radis
rag – un chiffon
rail (for trains) – un rail
  by train – par le train
railway – le chemin de fer
  French railways – S.N.C.F.

(Société Nationale des Chemins de fer Français)
rain – la pluie
  to rain – pleuvoir
  it is raining – il pleut
rainbow – un arc-en-ciel
raincoat – un imperméable
rainy – pluvieux
raisin – un raisin sec
ramble – une randonnée
  to go rambling – faire une randonnée
rapid – rapide
rapidly – rapidement
rare (of steak) – rare, saignant(e)
rash (careless) – imprudent(e)
  (medical) – une rougeur, une
  éruption
raspberry – une framboise
rat – un rat
rate (of exchange) – le taux de
  change
rather – plutôt
  I would rather leave – je
  préférerais partir
raw – cru(e)
razor – un rasoir
read (to) – lire
  I read – je lis
reading – la lecture
real – réel(le), véritable, vrai
really – vraiment
really? – c'est vrai?
rear – arrière
rear view mirror – un rétroviseur
reason – une raison
reasonable – raisonnable
receipt – un reçu
receive (to) – recevoir
  I receive – je reçois
recent – récent(e)

recently – récemment
reception (in a hotel) – la réception
  (welcome) – un accueil
recipe – une recette
record – un disque
record (to) – enregistrer
record player – un électrophone
red – rouge
red (hair) – (les cheveux) roux
red light (traffic) – un feu rouge
reel (fishing) – un moulinet
refrigerator – un frigo, un réfrigérateur, un frigidaire
refund – un remboursement
  to refund (money) – rembourser
refuse (to) – refuser
  I refuse – je refuse
refuse (rubbish) – les ordures (f pl)
region – une région
registration number – un numéro d'immatriculation
reimburse (to) – rembourser
relax (to) – se détendre
remain (to) – rester
remedy (for illness) – un remède
rendez-vous – un rendez-vous
repair (to) – réparer
repeat – répéter
  I repeat – je répète
  will you repeat that? – répétez, s'il vous plaît
replace (to) – remplacer
request – une demande
  to request – demander
rescue (to) – sauver
reservation – une réservation
reserve (to) – réserver

can I reserve a table? – je peux réserver une table?
rest (a) – le repos, une pause
  to rest – se reposer
restaurant – un restaurant
return (to) – revenir, rentrer, retourner
return ticket – un billet aller et retour
returns, many happy! – bon anniversaire!
reverse (back) – le dos, l'envers (m)
reward – une récompense
rheumatism – le rhumatisme
ribbon (hair) – un ruban
rich – riche
ride (a) – une promenade, un tour
  to ride – rouler
  to go for a ride – faire une promenade
right (not left) – à droite
  on the right – à droite
  (true) – juste, exact(e)
  right road – la bonne route
  (just, fair) – juste, équitable
  to be right – avoir raison
  you are right – vous avez raison
ring (jewellery) – une bague
ring (to) – sonner
  to ring up – téléphoner
  to ring back – rappeler
risk – un risque, un danger
river – une rivière
  (large) – un fleuve
road – une route
  (small) – un chemin
road map – une carte routière
road sign – un panneau de signalisation
roadway – la chaussée

road works – les travaux (m pl)
roast – un rôti
roast beef – un rôti de boeuf
rock (stone) – un rocher
rod (fishing) – une canne à pêche
roll (breakfast) – un petit pain
roof – un toit
roofrack – une galerie
room – une pièce
   (school) – une salle
   (space) – la place
roomy – spacieux, spacieuse
rope – une corde
rosemary (herb) – la romarin
rotten – pourri(e)
round – rond(e)
roundabout (road) – un rond-point
route – l'itinéraire (m)
R.S.V.P (reply please) – répondez s'il vous plaît
rubber (eraser) – une gomme
   made of rubber – en caoutchouc
rubbish – les ordures (f pl)
rubbish bin – une poubelle
rug – un petit tapis
ruin – une ruine
   to ruin – ruiner
   (spoil) – abîmer
ruler – une règle
run (to) – courir
rush (to) – se précipiter
rush hour – l'heure de pointe (f) (or d'affluence)

sad – triste
sadness – la tristesse
safe – en sécurité
safe and sound – sain et sauf
safely – sans danger, sans accident

safety – la sécurité
safety pin – une épingle de sûreté
sail (to go for a) – faire une promenade en bateau
sailing boat – un bateau à voiles
salad – une salade
salad bowl – un saladier
salad cream – une sorte de mayonnaise
salad dressing – la vinaigrette
sale – une vente
   (at reduced prices) – les soldes (m pl)
   for sale – à vendre
sales assistant – un vendeur, une vendeuse
salmon – un saumon
salt – le sel
salt cellar – une salière
same – même
   at the same time – en même temps
   all the same – quand même
sand – le sable
sand castle – un château de sable
sandal – une sandale
sandwich – un sandwich
sanitary (clean) – hygiénique
sanitary towel – une serviette hygiénique
sardine – une sardine
satisfactory – satisfaisant(e)
Saturday – samedi
sauce – la sauce
saucer – une soucoupe
sauna – un sauna
sausage – une saucisse
save (to) (a person) – sauver
   to save money – économiser
savings bank – une caisse d'épargne

say (to) – dire
scarf – une écharpe
  (square) – un foulard
scene – une scène
  (of accident) – un lieu, un endroit
scenery – le paysage
scent – le parfum, l'odeur (f)
school – une école
  (secondary) – un collège, un lycée
school child – un écolier, une écolière, un collégien, une collégienne
school teacher (primary) – un instituteur, une institutrice
  (secondary) – un/une professeur
science – la science
science fiction – la science fiction
scissors – des ciseaux (m pl)
Scotland – l'Ecosse (f)
Scottish – écossais, écossaise
screwdriver – un tournevis
sea – la mer (f)
  at the seaside – au bord de la mer
seafood – les fruits (m pl) de mer
seashore – le rivage, la plage, le bord de mer
seasickness – le mal de mer
seaside resort – une station balnéaire
season – une saison
seasonal – saisonnier, saisonnière
second (not first) – deuxième
second class – deuxième classe
second hand – d'occasion
second (in time) – une seconde
see (to) – voir
  I see – je vois

seesaw – un jeu de bascule
sellotape – le papier collant, le scotch
semi – semi, demi
semi-detached house – une maison jumelle
semi-final – une demi-finale
send (to) – envoyer
  I am sending you – je t'envoie
sentence – une phrase
September – septembre
septic – septique, infecté(e)
serial – un feuilleton
series – une série
serve (to) – servir
service – le service
  is the service included? – le service est compris?
service-station – une station-service
serviette – une serviette de table
settee – un divan, un canapé
seven – sept
severe – sévère, strict(e)
  (hard) – rigoureux, rigoureuse, dur(e)
sewage – les vidanges (f pl)
sewer – un égout
sewing machine – une machine à coudre
shade – l'ombre
  in the shade – à l'ombre
shallow – peu profond(e)
shampoo – le shampooing
shandy – une bière panachée
share (to) – partager
shark – un requin
sharp – tranchant(e), aigu(e), pointu(e)
shave (to have a) – se raser
shaving brush – un blaireau

shaving cream – la crème à raser
she – elle
sheep – un mouton
sheet (on bed) – un drap
  (sheet of paper) – une feuille
shelf – une étagère, un rayon
shellfish – un crustacé
sherry – le sherry
shine (to) – briller
ship – un bateau
  (large) – un navire
shirt – une chemise
shoddy – de mauvaise qualité
shoe – une chaussure, un soulier
shop – un magasin
shop assistant – un vendeur, une vendeuse
shopkeeper – un marchand, une marchande, un commerçant, une commerçante
shopping centre – un centre commercial
shop window – une vitrine
shore (of sea/lake) – le rivage, la rive
short – court(e)
shoulder – une épaule
shout – un cri
  to shout – crier
show (a) (theatre) – un spectacle
  (exhibition) – une exposition
show (to) – montrer
shower – une douche
shrimp – une crevette
Shrove Tuesday – Mardi Gras
shut (to) – fermer
shuttlecock – un volant de badminton
shy – timide
sick – malade
  to be sick – vomir

side – un côté
  at the side of – à côté de
sight – la vue
  in sight – visible
  out of sight – hors de vue
  to go sight seeing – faire du tourisme
sign – un signe
  (notice) – un panneau
sign (to) – signer
sign here – signez ici
signal – un signal
signal (to) (in a car) – mettre son clignotant
signature – une signature
signpost – un poteau indicateur
silence – le silence
silent – silencieux, silencieuse
silk – la soie
silly – stupide, sot, sotte, bête
silver – l'argent (m)
  made of silver – en argent
similar (to) – semblable (à)
simple – simple
since – depuis
sincere – sincère
sing (to) – chanter
single – seul(e), unique
  (not married) – célibataire
  (not double) – simple
single bed – un lit à une personne
single room – une chambre à une personne
single ticket – un billet simple
sir – monsieur
sister – une soeur
sister-in-law – une belle-soeur
sit down! – asseyez-vous!
site (camp) – un camping
sitting (of assembly etc.) – une séance

(in canteen) – un service
sitting-room – un salon
situation – une situation
six – six
size (of clothes) – la taille
   (of shoes) – la pointure
skate (a) – un patin
   to skate – patiner
skateboard – une planche à roulettes
skating (ice) – le patinage à glace
   (roller) – le patinage à roulettes
skating rink – une patinoire
skewer – une brochette
ski (to) – skier, faire du ski
skier – un skieur, une skieuse
skid (to) – déraper
skilful – habile, adroit(e)
skin – la peau
skinny – maigre
skirt – une jupe
sky – le ciel
sleep (to) – dormir
   I sleep – je dors
sleeve – une manche
slice – une tranche
slight (slim) – mince
   (trivial) – faible
   (small) – petit(e), léger, légère
slightly – un peu
slim – mince
   to slim – maigrir
slip (mistake) – une erreur
slip (to) – glisser
slipper – une pantoufle
slippery – glissant(e)
slot-machine – un distributeur automatique
slow – lent(e)
slowly – lentement
small – petit(e)

smart – élégant(e), chic
   (intelligent) – intelligent(e)
smash (to) – casser, briser
smell – une odeur
   to smell – sentir
   that smells good – ça sent bon
smile (a) – un sourire
   to smile – sourire
smoke – la fumée
   to smoke – fumer
smoked – fumé(e)
smooth – lisse
snack – un casse-croûte
snackbar – un snack bar
snake – un serpent
sneeze (to) – éternuer
snow – la neige
   to snow – neiger
so – donc
so big – si grand
soap – le savon
soccer – le football
sock – une chaussette
socket (electrical) – une prise de courant
soda – un soda
sofa – un canapé
soft – doux, douce
soft drink – une boisson non alcoolisée
softly – doucement
soil (earth) – le sol, la terre
sole (of shoe) – une semelle
   (fish) – une sole
   (only) – seul(e), unique
some – du (m), de la (f), des (pl)
somebody – quelqu'un
something – quelque chose
sometimes – quelquefois, parfois
son – le fils
soon – bientôt

see you soon – à bientôt
sore (painful) – douloureux, douloureuse
  it is sore – ça fait mal
sorry – désolé(e)
  I am sorry – je suis désolé(e), pardon, excusez-moi
sort – une sorte
  to sort – ranger
soup – la soupe, le potage
sour – aigre
south – le sud
souvenir – un souvenir
space – l'espace (m)
  (room) – une place
Spain – l'Espagne (f)
Spanish – espagnol(e)
speak (to) – parler
  I speak – je parle
spectacles – les lunettes (f pl)
speed – la vitesse
speed limit – la limitation de vitesse
spell (to) – épeler
  how do you spell it? – comment ça s'écrit?
spend (time) (to) – passer
  (money) – dépenser
spicy – piquant(e)
spider – une araignée
spinach – les épinards (m)
spin drier – une essoreuse
splendid – superbe, magnifique
sponge – une éponge
spoon – une cuiller
sport – le sport
spot – une tache
  (on pattern) – un pois
  (pimple) – un bouton
  (place) – un endroit, un coin
spring (season) – le printemps

sprouts (Brussels) – les choux (m pl) de Bruxelles
squalid – sordide
square (shape) – carré(e)
  (in a town) – une place
squirrel – un écureuil
stadium – un stade
stain – une tache
stairs – un escalier
stamp (postage) – un timbre
start (to) – commencer
start (of a race) – le départ
station – une gare
  (police etc.) – un poste
  (petrol) – une station-service
stay – un séjour
  to stay – rester
  I stay – je reste
steak – le bifteck
steep – raide
  (price) – très élevé(e)
step (a) – un pas
  (stair) – une marche
stew – le ragoût
stick – un bâton
sticky – adhésif, adhésive
stiff – raide, rigide, dur(e)
still – calme, tranquille
  (up to now) – encore, toujours
sting – une piqûre
stocking – un bas
stomach – le ventre, l'estomac (m)
stone – une pierre
stop (a) – un arrêt, une halte
  to stop – arrêter
storm – un orage, une tempête
stormy – orageux, orageuse
story – une histoire
straight – droit(e)
straight on – tout droit
stream – un ruisseau

street – une rue
strike – une grève
  to strike (hit) – frapper
string – ficelle
strip – une bande
  cartoon strip – une bande dess-
    inée
strong – fort(e)
student – un étudiant, une étudi-
  ante
study (to) – étudier
stupid – stupide, bête
subject (at school) – une matière
subscription – un abonnement
sub-title – un sous-titre
suburb – un faubourg
  the suburbs – la banlieue
subway – un passage souterrain
sudden – soudain
suddenly – soudain, tout à coup
suffer (to) – souffrir
  I am suffering – je souffre
sugar – le sucre
suit (a) – un costume, un complet
  (woman's) – un ensemble
suitcase – une valise
summer – l'été
sun – le soleil
sunbathe (to) – prendre un bain
  de soleil
Sunday – dimanche (m)
sunflower – un tournesol
sunglasses – des lunettes (f) de
  soleil
suntan oil – l'huile (f) solaire
super! – formidable!
superb – superbe, magnifique
supermarket – un supermarché
supper – le dîner
  (late) – le souper
sure – sûr(e), certain(e)

  (of course) – bien sûr
surfboard – une planche de surf
surfing – le surf
surname – le nom de famille
surprise – une surprise
surprising – surprenant(e)
surroundings – les environs (m pl)
sweater – un tricot, un pull
sweet (pudding) – un dessert
  (candy) – un bonbon
  (not sour) – doux, douce, su-
    cré(e)
  (pleasant) – agréable, gentil(le)
sweetcorn – le maïs doux
swim (to) – nager
swimming – la natation
switch (a) – un bouton
  to switch on – allumer
  to switch off – éteindre
syrup – le sirop

table – une table
tablet – un comprimé
  (for sucking) – une pastille
tail – une queue
take (to) – prendre
  I take – je prends
talc – le talc
talk (to) – parler
  I talk – je parle
tall – grand(e)
tangerine – une mandarine
tap (sink) – un robinet
  to tap (hit) – taper
tape-recorder – un magnétophone
tarragon – l'estragon (m)
tart – une tarte
taste – un goût
  to taste – goûter
tax – une taxe

tea – le thé
　(snack for children) – le goûter
　(evening meal) – le dîner
tea cup – une tasse à thé
team – une équipe
teapot – une théière
tear (to) – déchirer
tear (crying) – une larme
tea-towel – un torchon
teddy (bear) – un ours en peluche
teenager – un adolescent, une adolescente
teeth – les dents (f pl)
telephone – un téléphone
telescope – un téléscope
television – une télévision
　TV set – un poste de télévision
tell (to) – dire
　tell me – dites-moi
　(a story) – raconter
temperature – la température
　to have a temperature – avoir de la fièvre
ten – dix
tennis – le tennis
tennis ball – une balle de tennis
tennis court – un court de tennis
tennis racket – une raquette de tennis
tennis shoes – les chaussures (f pl) de tennis
tent – une tente
tepid – tiède
terrace – une terrasse
　(row of houses) – une rangée de maisons
terrible – terrible, atroce
　(weather) – affreux, affreuse, épouvantable
terrific – fantastique, incroyable, terrible

　(wonderful) – formidable
tetanus – le tétanos
thank (to) – remercier
　I thank you – je vous remercie
thank you – merci
the – le (m), la (f), les (pl)
theatre – un théâtre
theft – un vol
then (at that time) – alors, à ce moment-là
　(next) – puis, ensuite
there (place) – là, là-bas
there is (are) – il y a
therefore – donc
thermometer – un thermomètre
thermos flask – un thermos
thick – épais, épaisse
thief – un voleur
thin – mince, maigre
thing – une chose, un objet
things – les affaires (f pl)
think (to) – penser, croire
　I think – je pense, je crois
third – troisième
　(fraction) – un tiers
thirsty (I am) – j'ai soif
thirteen – treize
thirty – trente
this – ce (m), cet (m)
　(before a vowel) – cette (f)
thousand – mille
thousands of – des milliers de
three – trois
throat – la gorge
　sore throat – mal à la gorge
thumb – le pouce
thunder – le tonnerre
Thursday – jeudi
thyme – le thym
ticket – un billet
　(for bus, tube) – un ticket

tide – la marée
tidy (to) – ranger
  I tidy – je range
tie (a) – une cravate
till (shop) – une caisse
till (until) – jusqu'à
time – le temps
  (by clock) – l'heure (f)
  what time is it? – quelle heure
    est-il?
timetable – un horaire
  (school timetable) – un emploi
    du temps
tin (can) – une boîte
tin foil – le papier d'étain
tinned – en boîte
tip (end) – le bout
  (waiter's) – un pourboire
tissue (paper handkerchief) – un
  mouchoir en papier
to – à
toast – le pain grillé
toe – un doigt de pied, un orteil
together – ensemble
toilet – les toilettes (f pl)
toilet paper – le papier hygiénique
toilet water – l'eau (f) de toilette
toll – le péage
tomato – une tomate
tomorrow – demain
tongs – les pinces (f pl)
tongue – la langue
tonight – ce soir
too (also) – aussi
  (excessively) – trop
tool – un outil
tooth – une dent
  I have toothache – j'ai mal aux
    dents
toothbrush – une brosse à dents
toothpaste – le dentifrice

top (of mountain) – le sommet
  (of bar, cupboard etc.) – le des-
    sus
  (lid) – un couvercle
  on top of – sur
torch – une lampe de poche
touch (to) – toucher
  do not touch! – ne touchez pas!
tour – un tour, une visite
tourism – le tourisme
tourist – un/une touriste
tourist office – le syndicat d'initiative
towards – vers
towel – une serviette
tea towel – un torchon
tower – une tour
town – une ville
town centre – le centre de la ville,
  le centre-ville
town hall – l'hôtel de ville, la
  mairie
town plan – un plan de la ville
towrope – un câble de remorque
tow-truck – une dépanneuse
toy – un jouet
track (path) – un chemin, une
  piste
traffic – la circulation
traffic jam – un embouteillage
traffic lights – les feux (m pl) (de
  signalisation)
train – un train
travel (to) – voyager
travel agency – une agence de voy-
  ages
traveller – un voyageur, une voy-
  ageuse
travellers' cheque – un chèque de
  voyage
tray – un plateau

treasure – le trésor
treatment – le traitement
trip – un voyage, une excursion
trolley (supermarket) – un chariot
trouble – des difficultés (f pl), des
problèmes (m pl)
(worry) – des ennuis (m pl)
trousers – un pantalon
trout – une truite
truck – un camion
true – vrai(e), exact(e)
trunks – un maillot or un slip (de
bain)
T-shirt – un tee-shirt
Tuesday – mardi
tummy – le ventre
tuna – le thon
tunnel – un tunnel
tureen – une soupière
turn (to) – tourner
(to turn off) – éteindre
(to turn on) – allumer
twelve – douze
twenty – vingt
twice – deux fois
twice as much – deux fois plus
twin – un jumeau, une jumelle
two – deux
type (category) – un genre, une
espèce, une sorte
typewriter – une machine à écrire
typical – typique
tyre – un pneu
tyre pressure – la pression (des
pneus)

ugh! – pouah!
ugly – laid(e)
umbrella – un parapluie
unbearable – insupportable

under – sous
(less than) – moins de
understand (to) – comprendre
I do not understand – je ne
comprends pas
underwear – les sous-vêtements
(m pl)
undress (to) – se déshabiller
unfair – injuste
unfold (to) – déplier
unfortunate – malheureux, mal-
heureuse
unfriendly (cold) – froid(e),
inamical(e)
unhappy – triste
(dissatisfied with) – mécon-
tent(e) (de)
uniform (school) – un uniforme
scolaire
unique – unique
unkind – peu gentil(le)
unlucky (to be) – ne pas avoir la
chance
unmarried – célibataire
unplug (to) – débrancher
unsafe – dangereux, dangereuse,
hasardeux, hasardeuse
untidy – en désordre
until – jusqu'à
unwell – malade, souffrant(e)
upset (to) (disturb) – déranger
upside down – à l'envers
upstairs – en haut
up-to-date – moderne, très
récent(e)
urgent – urgent(e)
use – l'emploi (m), l'utilisation (f),
l'usage (m)
out of use – hors d'usage
to use – se servir de, utiliser,
employer

useful – utile
useless – inutile
utensil – un ustensile
kitchen utensils – une batterie de cuisine

vacancy (room) – une chambre disponible
vacant – libre, disponible
vacuum cleaner – un aspirateur
vacuum flask – un thermos
valuable – de grande valeur
value – la valeur
　V.A.T. – taxe (f) à la valeur ajoutée (T.V.A.)
van – une camionnette
vanilla – la vanille
varied – varié(e), divers(e)
variety – la variété
V.A.T. (*see value*)
veal – le veau
vegetable – un légume
vehicle – un véhicule
velvet – le velours
vending machine – un distributeur automatique
very – très
very much – beaucoup
vest – un tricot de corps
video (film) – une vidéo
video recorder – un magnétoscope
view – une vue
　(opinion) – l'avis (m)
village – un village
vine – une vigne
vinegar – le vinaigre
vineyard – un vignoble
visit – une visite
　(stay) – un séjour
　to visit (a place) – visiter

　(a person) – rendre visite à
voice – une voix
volleyball – le volleyball
vomit (to) – vomir
voyage – un voyage
　(sea crossing) – une traversée

wafer – une gaufrette
waffle – une gaufre
waist – la taille, la ceinture
Wales – le Pays de Galles
walk (a) – une promenade
　(short walk) – un petit tour
　to walk – marcher, aller à pied
　to go for a walk – se promener, faire une promenade
wall – un mur
wallet – un portefeuille
want (to) – vouloir
　I want – je veux
wardrobe – une armoire, une garde-robe
warm – chaud(e)
　it is warm weather – il fait chaud
　to warm (water) – chauffer
warmth – la chaleur
warn (to) – avertir, prévenir
warning triangle (for car) – un triangle de présignalisation
wash (to) – laver
　to wash oneself – se laver
　I have a wash – je me lave
　to wash up – faire la vaisselle
washable – lavable
washbowl – un lavabo
washing machine – une machine à laver
washing powder – la lessive
washing up liquid – un produit pour la vaisselle

washroom – les toilettes, le bloc sanitaire
wastepaper basket – une corbeille à papier
watch (clock) – une montre
watch (to) – regarder, observer
  (spy on) – surveiller
watch out! – attention!
water – l'eau (f)
  to water (plants) – arroser
waterproof – imperméable
wave (sea) – une vague
  (of hand) – un signe
  (radio) – une onde
  to wave (the hand) – agiter (la main)
way – un passage, la direction
  (manner) – la façon, la manière
  on the way – en route
weak – faible
  (health) – fragile
wear (to) – porter
Wednesday – mercredi
week – une semaine
weekend – le weekend
weekly – une fois par semaine
  (weekly magazine) – un hebdomadaire
weigh (to) – peser
weight – le poids
welcome (to) – accueillir
  you are welcome – bien venu(e)
  you're welcome (don't mention it) – de rien, il n'y a pas de quoi
well (good) – bien
  very well – très bien
wellingtons – les bottes (f pl) de caoutchouc
Welsh – gallois(e)

west – l'ouest (m)
wet – mouillé(e)
  (damp) – humide
  (soaked) – trempé(e)
  (rainy) – pluvieux
wheel – une roue
when – quand
where – où
whisky – le whisky
white – blanc, blanche
Whitsun – la Pentecôte
whole (complete) – entier, entière, tout(e)
  (not broken) – intact(e), complet, complète
why – pourquoi
wide – large, vaste
widow – une veuve
wife – une femme, une épouse
wild – sauvage
win (to) – gagner
  I've won! – j'ai gagné!
wind (weather) – le vent
  it's windy – il fait du vent
window – une fenêtre
  (shop window) – une vitrine
  (in a car, train) – une vitre
windscreen – un pare-brise
windscreen washer – un lave-glace
windscreen wiper – un essuie-glace
wine – le vin
wing – une aile
winter – l'hiver (m)
winter sports – les sports (m pl) d'hiver
wipe (to) – essuyer
wise – sage, prudent(e)
wish (a) – un désir
  best wishes – meilleurs voeux

to wish – désirer, vouloir
with – avec
without – sans
woman – une femme
wood (timber/small forest) – un bois
wooden – en bois
wool – la laine
woollen – en laine
word – un mot
  (spoken) – une parole
work – le travail
  to work – travailler
  I work – je travaille
  (to work mechanism) – marcher, fonctionner
  it doesn't work – ça ne marche pas
  out of work – au chômage
world – le monde
worried – inquiet, inquiète
worry (to) – s'inquiéter
  I am worried – je m'inquiète
worse – pire
worst – le (la) pire
wound (injury) – une blessure
wrist – le poignet
write (to) – écrire
  I write – j'écris
writing – l'écriture
wrong – faux, fausse

you are wrong! – vous avez tort!
what's wrong? – qu'est-ce qu'il y a?
yacht – un voilier, un yacht
yard – une cour
year – un an, une année
yearly – annuel(le)
yellow – jaune
yes – oui
yesterday – hier
yesterday morning – hier matin
yet – encore
yoghurt – le yaourt
you – tu (singular and informal), vous (polite form and plural)
young – jeune
your – ton (m), ta (f), tes (pl)
  (polite form) – votre, vos (pl)
youth – la jeunesse
youths – les jeunes
youth club – une maison des jeunes
youth hostel – une auberge de jeunesse

zero – zéro (m)
zip (fastener) – une fermeture éclair
zone – une zone, un secteur
zoo – un zoo
zoom (lens) – un zoom

Index